LEAVING HOME

DAVID P. CELANI

LEAVING HOME

The Art of Separating from Your Difficult Family

COLUMBIA UNIVERSITY PRESS

NEW YORK

Columbia University Press
Publishers Since 1893
New York   Chichester, West Sussex
Copyright © 2005 Columbia University Press
All rights reserved

Library of Congress Cataloging-in-Publication Data

Celani, David P.
Leaving home : the art of separating from your difficult family / David P. Celani.
p. cm.
Includes bibliographic references and index
ISBN 978-0–231–13476–7 (cloth : alk. paper)
1. Adult children—United States. 2. Adult children of dysfunctional families—United States.
3. Separation (Psychology) 4. Self-help techniques. I. Title.
HQ799.97.U5C45 2005
306.874—dc22   2004051980

Printed in the United States of America

c 10 9 8 7 6 5 4 3 2

For Barbara

CONTENTS

ACKNOWLEDGMENTS

I wish to express my appreciation to the many individuals who offered help and support during the writing of this book. Special thanks goes to Stephen Krupa, who offered an insightful critique of the work as well as enthusiasm and encouragement. Thanks also goes to Robert Barasch, Ph.D., who likewise was helpful with his comments and suggestions. I am also indebted to my two editors, Leonora Gibson at Wesleyan University Press, who offered direction and support at the outset of the project, and John Michel at Columbia University Press, who brought the project to fruition. Finally, I again express my appreciation to my wife, Veronica, who has been a constant source of encouragement throughout my career.

LEAVING HOME

INTRODUCTION

One of the very first patients I worked with was a young athletic trainer who bore a striking resemblance to Robert Redford. At first glance, I couldn't imagine what could be troubling to such a handsome and graceful young fellow, although I was soon convinced that he was indeed in need of my help, as he was plagued by recurring depressions. This surprised me, because his youth and robust appearance gave him an air of confident well-being. However, as he began to describe his life to me, I became convinced that he had every reason to be depressed. He had been raised by cold and uncaring parents who appeared perfectly normal to those outside of the family. His mother kept a clean house and served well-prepared food, but behind closed doors she demonstrated little interest in or emotional attachment to her son. She spent every afternoon watching soap operas, and my patient soon learned not to disturb her when he came home from school. He spent much of his time in his room building plastic models of ships and planes. Similarly, his father appeared on the surface to be a good father, in that he was both dependable and a good provider, yet he was almost completely unresponsive to his son's emotional needs. My patient characterized his childhood experience as like living in a "private and secret orphanage." He assumed that his parents ignored him because he had some defect that was obvious to them, and as time passed he felt more and more inferior and self-conscious.

When he reached his teenage years, his father announced that he would teach him about the outdoors. This surprised my patient, since up to this time his father had behaved as if his son barely existed. Father and son went hunting and fishing, but instead of enjoying the unusual attention focused on him, my patient recalled these "lessons" as sheer torture. He was already ill at ease with both parents because the years of emotional rejection made him extremely sensitive to criticism, since he assumed he was somehow "damaged goods." His father was an expert woodsman, but instructed him very sparsely—but still expected his timid and fearful son to know what to do under pressure. For example, when they went deer hunting, his father would follow his progress in the woods from several yards back, critiquing his skills by clapping his hands if he did something wrong. Every time he stepped on a twig that made a noise, it would be followed by a loud handclap. The mounting pressure from his silent and critical father made him so nervous and self-conscious that when he finally sighted his first deer, he was paralyzed by the fear that he would make another mistake. His hands began to tremble so severely that he could not even lift his gun. His father began clapping his hands and the deer bounded off in the distance. Similarly, when fishing from a small boat, he panicked when he hooked his first fish, not knowing which way to crank the fishing reel. He looked to his father for help and saw a man whose face was red with rage and frustration. His father began clapping his hands again, and my patient, filled with fear, threw the fishing rod into the lake.

The fishing incident convinced his father to abandon all attempts to usher his son into adulthood. Soon after, his father handed him a carefully worded letter that said that he was a great disappointment as a son, and that he would no longer take him hunting or fishing. Nothing was ever mentioned verbally about the letter and the "family" continued on as if nothing had happened.

As a young man, he went to college and excelled both academically and athletically. Not surprisingly, his social life was constricted and unsatisfactory, as his sense of inferiority made him exceedingly shy around women of his age. He was jealous of his roommate and friends who had normal and easy relationships with women. He assumed that they were successful because of their physical "builds," so my patient began a program of bodybuilding. His increased musculature did little to attract female students, so he concluded that his lack of success was due to a clique that deliberately excluded him. He had no ability to see that his painful shyness and envy were felt by his peers and caused his social failures.

After graduation, he decided to see the country before starting his job as a athletic trainer. He joined an organized cross-country bicycle expedition with twenty-five other similarly adventuresome peers. He considered the three-month trip to be a complete success, yet my patient decided to purchase a home right next door to his parents' house soon after he began working that fall. Not surprisingly, the proximity to his parents had terrible consequences, as he was drawn into their increasingly frequent arguments. Typically, he would return home from his job and begin preparing dinner, only to be interrupted by a "distress signal" from next door. His mother would flash the living room lights on and off and my patient would drop everything and run to help her. The battle between my patient's parents finally culminated in his mother's threat to move next door—to my patient's house—in retribution for the verbally abusive treatment she was receiving from her husband. Ever since my patient left home, his father's critical focus had been turned on his mother, who had become a social isolate and constant television watcher. My patient's role in this sad family scenario was to make peace between his embittered and resentful parents, a task which usually took several hours. By the time he was able to return to his own home he would be too upset to finish his dinner. This constant gut-wrenching involvement in his parents' battles, and his stalled life (how could he bring a woman home with the possibility of a battle next door?) provoked the frequent depressions that led him to seek therapy.

After he described his childhood, I asked him with exaggerated curiosity just how it was possible that the most interesting house he saw on his three-month bicycle trip *just happened to be right next door* to his parents' home? He had no explanation other than the fact that he wanted to visit his mother for breakfast. His decision ignored the reality that he had recognized—long before he bought the house—that his parents had become disagreeable to each other and to him.

This clinical example illustrates a classic psychological scenario that is repeated all too frequently: an attractive, educated, and capable adult who was poorly nurtured and is consequently unable to separate from the very parents who neglected him in childhood. This book will address the question of why some young adults are able to launch themselves confidently into life while others remain at home, hardly venturing out, fearful of the world, and discontented with their lives—yet completely unable to change. We all know examples of bright and attractive young adults who, despite all the advantages of education, cannot leave home and start a family of their own. Nearly every family has one middle-aged relative who is still living with his or her elderly parents and despite obvious unhappiness is unable to separate and live on his or her own. In other cases, the young adult manages to leave the family home but remains a slave to their parents' every opinion, often calling home daily or visiting for meals, while neglecting other adult relationships. Our culture often labels immature male adults who are overly attached to their mothers as "mama's boys"—however, either gender can become unhealthily mired in their family of origin.

Leaving your family, particularly if they failed to meet your childhood needs, is the hardest psychological task in adult life. The paradox that this book will explore is the unexpected observation that children who are loved and nurtured in childhood have a relatively easy time leaving home and starting their own families, while children who were ignored, neglected, or even abused are much less able to leave the very home that failed them. Adult logic would suggest that the reverse would be true: that the loved child would remain close to his or her parents in order to continue to enjoy the rewards of relating to loving parents, while the neglected young adult would flee and avoid his depriving parents at all cost.

Giving up on one's family, no matter how negative, is not an action that is received well in our culture. We are told by pop psychology books to "make peace with our parents" or to "forgive" them for what they did to us when we were young and vulnerable. Many organized religions tell us to respect and honor our parents regardless of how they treated us as children. As we will see, the apparently simple act of choosing to separate from one's family of origin is seen by many as an offense against our social and religious fabric. Many opponents will condemn the individual who takes this action, even when it is taken in adulthood. Most prominent of the naysayers will be the neglectful parents themselves, who will feel enormously threatened when their adult child begins to separate. Many will use the shopworn cliche that "blood is thicker than water" as an attempt to avoid any change that would alter long-term dysfunctional patterns.

Giving up our attachment to our hurtful family means giving up both our hope for and our guilty concern about our family of origin. The individual who takes this self-protective action exposes himself to an enormous taboo, and I intend this book to serve as a source of support for those who choose this path. Separation from one's dysfunctional family is essential for the mental health of the individual, as it signals the transition from childhood to adulthood. I hope to offer a clearly reasoned and logical pathway to freedom to adults who are ensnared by their negative family. The alternative is to remain attached to the family, either in actuality (by remaining single and living in the family home) or symbolically, through the re-creation of similar abusive, rejecting, and demeaning adult relationships. Sadly, both choices leave us in a state of suspended animation, forever waiting to start an authentic new life of our own.

The purpose of this book is to outline a quiet and reasonable program for the reader who is interested in separating from his or her family. I hope to demonstrate the essential and life-saving nature of this task, as well as the steps that help one to succeed at this difficult psychological endeavor. Conversely, this book is not designed to encourage the reader to engage in endless dramatic (and ultimately futile) recriminations against his or her failed parents. We currently have many popular psychology television programs that urge their guests to detail every memory of neglect or abuse. Often, these recitations of victimization become an end in themselves, as they offer temporary empathy from a sympathetic audience, but they do not promote moving on in life. Rather, they encourage the individual to become a professional "victim" whose most important achievement in life is the retelling of the original abuse.

The purpose of this book is to outline a quiet and reasonable program for the reader who is interested in separating from his or her family. I hope to demonstrate the essential and life-saving nature of this task, as well as steps that help one to succeed at this difficult psychological endeavor.

I am first going to look at the issue of destructive human attachments from the very beginning of the first human relationship: the child's relationship to the mother and father. Many of the "classic" self-help books enter a complex and lengthy drama in the third act (that is, adulthood) and try to guess what happened in the opening act. My approach begins by examining faulty emotional attachments from their foundation in childhood, and then connect that early faulty pattern of relating to the adult's inability to separate from the same family that failed to meet his needs in childhood.

The Psychological Foundation of *Leaving Home*

This book, despite its clear and understandable language and its lack of jargon, is based on a longstanding psychoanalytic model that has existed since 1940 and has grown in importance over the last twenty years. The field of psychoanalysis is not a single model or theory, but rather comprises a group of similar theories that compete with one another and are based in "schools" or analytic institutes that specialize in one model or another. The closest analogy is Protestantism: a group of churches that share fundamental beliefs, but that differ in emphasis and religious ritual.

All psychoanalytic theories (there are five major schools of thought) originated with Freud, who was the titan of the field. Each of the models evolved and moved away from Freud's concepts, but they all share the view that the human unconscious is the primary motivator of human behavior. They differ widely in their understanding of how the unconscious develops and operates. The psychoanalytic model on which *Leaving Home* is based is called "Object Relations Theory," which is a model that evolved out of Freud's original writings, but that differs markedly with most of Freud's theory (currently referred to as "classical psychoanalysis"). Freud's model was an instinct or "drive" model—he assumed that all human motivation originated in primitive instincts that were based on either sex or aggression. He called this fundamental human motivation "libido," and he assumed that it operated from birth. The sexual motivation felt by the infant toward his or her mother would now be called tenderness or pleasure from reduction of hunger. Freud referred to the mother of the infant as the "sexualized object" and over the years, the careful study of relationships between mothers and infants began to be referred to as "object relationships." This is the origin of the name of the branch of psychoanalysis that this book is based upon, an unfortunate name because humans outside of ourselves are referred to as "objects."

Freud lived at the dawn of the scientific revolution and he freely borrowed concepts from Darwin, the most successful scientist of his time. Prior to Darwin, the only "model of man" was religious creationism, and Darwin challenged all of religion with his discovery of evolutionary biology. This shift of concepts away from religion and toward scientific explanation of humankind was far greater than anything we have seen in our generation. Freud was so impressed with the power of science and the view of humanity that Darwin's theory offered that he incorporated Darwin's concepts into his psychological model. In Freud's model, primitive instincts were given the central role as providers of all human motivation. These instincts were the psychological equivalents of Darwin's concept of our humanoid ancestors that existed before modern man. Freud gave life to these primitive ancestors in our mental life by

assuming that they still existed in the humans of today. He proposed that each of us contained a mental construct that he called
the "id," which is an unconscious cauldron of drives that pressed
upward, seeking conscious expression. Thus Freud's id was the psychological equivalent of Darwin's primitive early man, and he assumed that it was the power source for the entire personality. No
child could survive in its family with only the ruthless behavior that
characterizes the id, and Freud solved this problem by introducing
his second personality structure, the "ego." Freud's ego was a part
of the id (the original power source), but it modified itself and developed into a "go-between," mediating between the unconscious
id and the society's demands. The ego was not a "self" as we now
understand the concept of a multifaceted human identity, but
rather a puppet that served the primitive needs of the id while trying to remain within the confines of cultural demands. The fundamental conflict in humankind according to classical psychoanalysis
is always the same—a constant struggle between the id's aggressive
and sexual motivation and the restrictions imposed by society.
Freud also accounted for the "higher" characteristics of humankind including altruism, love, religious conviction, and social
responsibility with his third psychic structure, and the last one to
develop in the child, which he called the "superego." Freud postu-
lated that the superego evolved from "internalization" of the attitudes and standards set forth by the child's parents and others who
conveyed the rules of society. The development of the superego was
the point in Freud's theory from which Object Relations Theory developed. Had Freud been consistent in his theory building, he
would have insisted that the superego evolve out of the ego, since
his model was purely "instinctual." All his psychological structures
should have evolved from inherited biological instincts. But Freud
erred and created a "mixed" model, akin to welding the front of a
Ford and the rear of a Plymouth together. The origin of his superego emerges from a different (noninstinctual) and competing
process. That is, an alternative view of personality development is
that our sense of self or identity evolves from social interactions
that are stored in memory. This view produces a very different, and

in many ways an *opposite* psychological model. Taken further, the "internalization" model of personality development sees the formation of the human personality not as the unfolding of primitive drives, but rather as the accumulation of memories of one's parents in relationship to oneself, which eventually forms a "self."

The process by which this second psychoanalytic model developed took many years and was begun by Melanie Klein, a loyal follower of Freud. Klein did not realize that she was offering the world an alternative psychoanalytic model that would ultimately overtake classical Freudian thought. Klein was a German analyst who fled fascism to England. She considered herself a classical Freudian, but her writings emphasized the role of "internalized objects," that is, memories of the parents who both populated and exerted control of the child's developing personality. She saw the influence of these internalized objects as coexisting with Freud's drive theory. Again, this was a mixed model, but at the very dawn of psychoanalysis those in the field were so excited by the unfolding possibilities that pointed criticism of their model building was ignored. Klein's model exists today as one of the five major psychoanalytic models.

The next theorist who contributed to the development of Object Relations Theory was Ronald Fairbairn, and his theory of personality development is the model upon which this book is based. Fairbairn was a Scottish philosopher, physician, and psychoanalyst who wrote a series of papers outlining his model of the human personality in the 1940s. He took Klein's ideas a step further by eliminating all notions of biologically inherited drives and replaced them with a purely relational model. Fairbairn saw the human personality as constructed from thousands of conscious and unconscious memories of the child in interaction with his or her "objects," that is, his or her parents. His model is elegant, powerful, and completely understandable, and it highlights the critical importance of early childhood experiences. Fairbairn's unconscious is central to his model, but it is a very different unconscious than Freud's. Freud's unconscious had to remain repressed because it was too antisocial and violent for modern man to accept—it was, in other words, the primitive man within us. Fairbairn's unconscious was populated by memories of actual events: failures in parenting, hurts, and instances of abandonment that the child could not consciously tolerate. Thus both Freud and Fairbairn placed the unconscious at the center of their models, but the role and contents of their respective unconsciousnesses differ greatly.

The most important concept that Fairbairn proposed was the concept of "attachment to bad objects," which describes the abandoned, abused, or neglected child's intense loyalty to the very parent or parents who failed him or her. Fairbairn developed this concept in the years between 1927 and 1935, while he worked in an orphanage in Edinburgh. His model focuses on the plight of children who are completely dependent on parents (as we all were) who failed to meet their legitimate developmental needs. He noted that these children defended their abusive parents at all costs and could not wait to return to their physically abusive homes.

Fairbairn also enhanced our understanding of the Freudian concept of "repetition compulsion," the observation that humans paradoxically relive and re-create painful situations from their childhood in their adulthood relationships. Freud observed these same patterns, but his model of pleasure seeking (libido theory) had no way of explaining "pain seeking." He attempted to do so late in life with the drive concept of "thanatos" or the death instinct, which turned out to be his least accepted concept. Fairbairn understood repetition compulsion as the inevitable replay of the painful relationships that populate our unconscious. We seek others to act out roles that we took in our family of origin, or those that were originally taken by one or the other of our parents. Repetition compulsion is neither pain seeking or pleasure seeking, but rather a re-creation of our original family that has become the internal template of human relations that we have not been able to escape. We re-create the only relational world that we have ever known—one that is often biased toward frustration, longing, anger, and despair.

The positions that are taken in this book have a solid foundation. Fairbairn's observations are not "secrets" that are limited to the rarified world of psychoanalysis, but rather observations that have been independently noted by writers, essayists, and students of human behavior, many of whom I quote. The process of separation from one's family of origin for many adults raised in an atmosphere of neglect is both painful and difficult, but it is simultaneously an essential and life-affirming quest.

A Note on Confidentiality

This book contains many clinical examples taken from actual experiences from my twenty-six year career as a clinical psychologist. All the clinical conflicts that I describe are real; however, I have changed many of the personal characteristics of the patients in order to protect their privacy. Some examples are the result of mixing the characteristics of two patients together, while others are not. In some cases, I have obtained permission to use the material with little or no changes, and these are mixed in with others that have been modified. The goal is to give the reader a vivid and accurate window into the private world of psychotherapy without compromising the privacy of those who have participated in the change process.

ONE

The Building Blocks of Our Personality

Give me the child for the first seven years and he will be mine for
the rest of his life.

—*Jesuit maxim*

During my career as a clinical psychologist, I discovered that my
best teachers were always my patients, since they illustrated just
how the human personality developed and operated. One of the
finest was "George," a student from a private high school who was
sent for therapy with me by his mother and by his school as a last
resort before he was expelled. My task was to discover the reasons
behind George's habit of stealing from faculty members. He was an
earnest and appealing young man who had a talent for mathemat-
ics and physics and had also proven to be an outstanding hockey
player. He was assumed to be a prize student until it was discovered that wherever he went, items were found to be missing. In particular, he stole faculty members' wallets, purses, date books, and
other personal items. George reported in his wide-eyed way that he
had no idea why he had such sticky fingers, though he did sense a
thrill of victory when he examined the items he stole. He did not
spend the money he took—rather, he returned the stolen items in
odd ways. For instance, he would take a stolen wallet and drop it
down a laundry chute, or leave it on a hallway floor where it could
be found by someone else. After our first clinical interview, I felt a

sense of certainty that I could work with George, but was flustered when I could not find a roll of stamps that had been clearly visible on my desk. George had managed to deftly lift them as he exited my office. I was equally surprised to find the same roll of stamps encircling the antenna on my car as I left my office later that evening. Clearly, George was involved in some sort of game, one that produced the uncanny feeling that I was the vulnerable one, and that George had maneuvered himself into a superior position. During the next weeks, George and I explored his history and I became ever more alert to the items in my office, but George managed, by sheer genius and single-mindedness of purpose, to take a number of them. I encountered a good number of pens, my stationery, a book, and a decorative item or two in the parking lot, on top of the garbage can (how appropriate), or on the lawn. I felt that George, who was supposed to be a patient seeking help, was actually demonstrating that he was "one-up" on me, an allegedly "helpful" authority figure.

I began to explore his childhood history and found that he was raised in a single-parent family that was generally supportive with the exception of dinnertime. His mother was extremely strict about eating—especially vegetables—and had rules that were non-negotiable and often brought her into conflict with George, who was the older of her two children. When food was put in front of him, George was expected to eat it, regardless of his preferences. If he refused, his mother would impose a series of increasingly severe punishments. At first, his mother would require him to sit at the table until he ate. However, as he got older and older, George found out that he could out-wait his mother. Not infrequently, they both ended up sitting at the table for two hours, George stubbornly refusing to eat, while his mother sat angrily enforcing her rules. It soon became apparent to his mother that she was as trapped as her son, because she had to remain at the table in the role of enforcer. She devised a plan which imposed a time limit on each meal with punishments that would take place in the future. For instance, if he refused to eat his portion within fifteen minutes, he lost his allowance for the following week. Longer periods of refusal invoked more severe punishments, including being barred from visiting friends, loss of future birthday gifts, and restriction of his telephone privileges. A large calendar was marked far into the future with the restrictions and punishments that he had accumulated for his stubborn refusal to eat.

When George was seven, he began rummaging through his mother's purse and took great pride in stealing change from her. He realized that if he were caught, more punishments would be forthcoming, so he was very careful to take small amounts of change that would not be missed. He also took his mother's car keys and placed them in a spot where she would be frustrated yet unable to blame him. She would often be late and frantically looking for her keys, only to discover them on the garage floor or next to the kitchen sink. Interestingly, George's younger sister was also subject to the same rules at the dinner table, but she adopted the compliant role, and therefore all the pressure and conflict was focused on George.

The pattern of attachment that developed between George and his mother was one between a dominant and implacable mother who treated him in an insensitive and autocratic manner. There simply was no healthy reason for this mother to treat her children this way. However, like most parents, she probably believed that she was doing the correct thing, even if it was a repetition of an unconscious destructive pattern that she experienced in her own childhood. Had I been able to question George's mother (which I never did), I am quite certain that she would defend her severe training of her children, saying that was in their best interests. She might claim that she was teaching her children to eat all types of food for a balanced diet, or perhaps that she was teaching them healthy discipline.

A student of mine who heard this example in class suggested that the problem at the dinner table was this young George's fault! Specifically, the student said that it was his stubborn refusal to eat that caused the problem with his mother. This reaction demonstrates the tendency to "blame the victim" and more importantly, it ignores critical information about the psychological development of the human personality. George's refusal to eat was not just "stubbornness"—rather, it was the only way he had of preserving his sense of himself and his identity in the face of his mother's overwhelming power. He was trapped by his human needs: he had to eat, and he could not dine anywhere else. His normal and expectable human needs were turned against him by the most important person in the world: his mother. He and his sister were totally dependent on their mother, as their father was not in the picture, like many millions of children today. They could not stop eating and they could not get a different mother. They simply had to adapt as best they could.

If George's refusal to eat is more than simple stubbornness, what is it? There is another human need—a need as important as the need to eat—that was continually violated by his mother: his need for his individuality to be accepted and respected. George's relationship with his mother taught him that his individual taste in food was not important and it had to be forcibly subordinated to his mother's will. This was exacerbated by the fact that his mother would often provoke him by deliberately serving a variety of his most hated vegetables. His refusal to eat is the only way he could define himself in this situation. When he was forced to eat something that he did not like, he was giving up his position as an individual by accepting his mother's demand that he eat whatever she put on the table, regardless of his personal preference.

Every time he gave in to his mother's dominance, he simultaneously gave up his own individuality and experienced strong emotions of both humiliation and shame. We all faced numerous humiliations in childhood: failures at school, rejections from peers, and the difficulties inherent in doing many things at which we have limited natural talent. Generally, parents try to cushion the humiliations suffered by their children, but George had a mother who humiliated him within what should have been the "safe zone" of his own family. His solution to this growing anger at being humiliated was to steal. It was a perfect form of revenge, as he could enjoy secret victories over his mother and yet not be punished for them as long as they were cleverly disguised.

The struggle between George and his mother became and more painful as he grew older, because like all developing children, his sense of himself as an individual became stronger over time. The older he got, the more his sense of self felt compromised when he was forced to give in. By the time George was sixteen, the struggle had changed. He had developed an enormously angry, creative, and devious personality, and he had put in place a whole series of alternative dinnertime venues that neatly sidestepped his mother's rules. He would secretly eat at the houses of his friends, where he was careful to ingratiate himself with his friends' mothers. He also had several hidden stashes of food both in his room and in the garage, so he could secretly defy his mother while simultaneously maintaining his self-respect.

However, when he was six, there were no alternatives—no meals at friend's homes and no stashes of chips to dampen his hunger and help defy his mother's rules. These excessively painful humiliations was the primary source of damage to George's personality, making him deeply ashamed of his weakness and wary of closeness with others. However, his strategies for revenge against his mother constituted a second and more destructive type of damage to his personality. The secondary damage to his personality came from his "solutions" (his stealing and stubbornness) to his mother's dominance. George might have succeeded in young adulthood if he had been able to shed his damaged personality (both his feelings of humiliation and his revenge behaviors) the moment he left home, but the human personality is like the shell of the turtle: we take it everywhere we go.

It was the second aspect of the damage to George's personality (his revenge strategies) that became the problem for George after he left his home. His strategies for dealing with his intrusive mother were very important to him, as they helped to preserve his developing identity during his difficult childhood. In many ways, his creative strategy was like a parachute: in childhood, his solutions saved his self-respect, but in adulthood the same solutions, when applied to new people in parental roles, hindered him just as a tangled parachute on the ground can catch in the wind and drag the jumper to his death. In young adulthood, George couldn't give up his revenge-based solution to his mother's dominance because it was woven deeply into the fabric of his personality. All the insight from therapy, all his desire to change, and all the punishments heaped upon him had no effect on his stealing.

The Key Conflict:
Love and Anger Toward the Same Parent

George, like many children, was caught in an unsolvable conflict because his mother, whom he loved and needed desperately, was the very person wielding power against him in a destructive manner. This paradox added an important level of complexity to his emotional response to his mother. The repeated dinnertime struggle created feelings of anger and fear toward his mother, yet at other times he loved and needed her. The emotional tug-of-war between the opposite emotions of love and anger toward the same parent produces a fundamental conflict within all children who are exposed to parental tyranny or neglect. One moment, George was filled with anger toward his mother, and soon after dinner was over, he returned to needing and loving her once again. The endless conflict between love and anger is one of emotional tangles that bind adults to their rejecting families. Many adults who were raised with this conflict cannot hold a single emotional perspective toward their parents for any length of time. The moment they feel a clear feeling that would allow them to act decisively, it is replaced by an opposite feeling. For instance, one moment they may be enraged by their parent and then—almost instantaneously—feel overwhelmed by pity and sadness about the same parent. These shifting emotional sands prevent them from separating from the family as they are continually dragged back by their emotional confusion. No single course of action is open to them. This key point will be revisited in chapter 5.

In sharp contrast to George's family, a loving and functional family allows and encourages their children to define themselves by their natural skills: perhaps by success in a school play, sports, or academics. All of these are positive, self-enhancing building blocks that ultimately add up to a clear identity. Healthy parents exaggerate the success of their young children, often announcing their child's success to relatives who join in the praise. These early layers of memories become the unconscious foundation of the developing child's identity and they are essential later in life when inevitable difficulties require strength to overcome. We often label individuals who are able to overcome obstacles in life and ignore setbacks as being strong and having good "character," which is the happy result of good early parenting. Sensitive parents also allow the child to "lead" by observing their child's strengths and encouraging them in those areas. This requires that the parents be ready to sacrifice a great deal of their own time and freedom to support to their developing child.

The child raised in a healthy family takes in not only these positive memories of support but the countless repetitions of family scenes that inform him how to conduct his life, what is acceptable in relationships to parents and siblings, how to behave at social events, and countless other details that together form a large part of the child's identity. Just as chaos and family dysfunction is passed from one generation to the next, so is healthy functioning, which is based on family relationships that foster trust, respect for each individual, and deep emotional attachment toward members of the family.

Another characteristic of healthy parenting is the existence of an often unspoken family plan or philosophy of life that guides the actions of the parents and lends a seamless organization to all family activities. Healthy family "plans" always include nurturing the children so they can begin their lives with skills and with a sense of how they should organize their lives. They may include having all the children go to college, or become members of one or another religious community, or become art lovers, businessmen, or serve in politics. Less healthy family philosophies that are transmitted to children may include grooming the children to be socially prominent, wealthy, or famous, without concern for others. However, even an unhealthy plan offers the child a long-term view of life and some sense of family organization. The least healthy family, developmentally speaking, is one with no long-term plans and no sense of organization or continuity. It is obvious why this last type of family is most damaging. As we have seen, the child's personality is developed by memories of similar events that are repeated time after time. Constant chaos and unpredictability within the family disrupts the organization of a sense of self in relation to others, as there are not enough consistent interpersonal events for a single unified sense of self to emerge. As we will see with numerous examples, many parents had developmental histories that did not allow their own personality to mature or develop normally. They never experienced a family with a coherent plan and predictable daily organization, thus leaving them with a constant sense of emptiness and need that does not give them the capacity to give up their time and energy to help in the development of their own children.

Unfortunately, my patient George was a child who did not have the good fortune to live in a family attuned to his developmental needs, nor did he have a mother with a larger plan in mind for George's future. Rather, her focus was on forcing her son to obey her demands, and consequently the most powerful events of personality building in George's childhood were the creative and ingenious strategies that he developed during the angry struggles with his mother at the dinner table. In his family, he and his sister had only two possible pathways to define who they were in relation to their mother: they could either be rebels or clones. Adults often assume children are "resilient," and are not affected by childhood difficulties, but in reality, the very core of George's personality was formed by both the repeated humiliations he experienced at his mother's hands and by his counteraggressive strategies. Together, they charted the course of the development of his personality.

The Development of the "Wounded Self"

Over a number of years, the childhood events that George experienced at the dinner table produced a "wounded self" within his larger personality. This is the first major defense mechanism of childhood, and its creation allows the child to remain attached to his parents who have either neglected or abused him. Loss of the attachment to the parent plunges the child into the terror of abandonment. Consequently, all defense mechanisms of the personality have the same goal, which is to keep the vulnerable child oblivious to the rejection he is experiencing and thus allow his sense of attachment to continue. If children raised in difficult and unnurturing families were somehow stripped of their defense mechanisms and could directly experience the reality of emotional abandonment, it would be analogous to dropping a five-year-old off in an unfamiliar city and driving away. All defense mechanisms work to help the child avoid experiencing the feeling of abandonment.

Every mealtime plunged George into a world of powerful expectations: memories and feelings of hundreds of past dinners where he experienced anger at his mother for setting up an impossible situation and anger toward himself for his weakness when he gave into her demands. Over time these intense feelings were formed into a large "package" within his developing personality that included feelings of hurt, humiliation, and rage. Each dinner added more memories to this growing package. These hundreds of separate but similar memories evolved into a sense of himself that is called the "wounded self." Specifically, George's wounded self was a sense of himself in a grim contest of wills with his mother at the dinner table: a sense of himself that was filled with impotence, anger, and a feeling of being trapped by a mother he (at other times) loved.

All children who develop a wounded self do so in order to remain attached to their neglectful or indifferent parent. The wounded self allows the child to stay attached to the needed parent first by "packaging" all the memories of humiliation and neglect in a single and distinct container, much like a computer file, and then by closing the file by burying (repressing) it in the unconscious the moment the abuse or neglect ends. The moment dinner ended, George would repress the painful package of memories of humiliation by his mother in his unconscious and then return to loving and needing his "good" mother the rest of the evening. The defense mechanism of repression allowed George's attachment to his mother (and thus his sense of security) to continue without being endangered by his angry feelings. Thus, during most of the time, George's wounded self remained hidden in his unconscious and allowed him to avoid the powerful feelings of anger and vulnerability that it contained. No six-, seven-, or eight-year-old child can cope with constant feelings of anger toward his desperately needed mother and at the same time cope with equally painful contempt for his own weakness. Thus, away from the dinner table George was able to relate to his mother in a loving manner, with his emotional attachment to her intact. Repression of the wounded self is every child's automatic solution to the problem of staying emotionally attached to a urgently needed parent who either deliberately (or inadvertently) frustrates his reasonable developmental needs. One of the most dramatic examples of a child defending against the reality of abuse is in Christine Lawson's book *Understanding the Borderline Mother*. She describes the following short scene: "A toddler whose mother slapped him across the face looked at his mother and exclaimed 'Somebody hit me!' " (139) This example shows how the child avoids the reality that undeserved abuse is coming from the person most needed, and the earliest defense mechanism of all—denial—is used to protect himself from an awareness that he simply could not tolerate.

The struggle between George and his mother was not really about food; it was a struggle between a child trying to defend his developing sense of self from his mother who was intent on crushing it. As he got older, George's wounded self became more apparent, as it manifested itself in his stealing from authority figures who meant him no harm. Kathryn Harrison, the author of the powerful memoir *The Kiss*, described her awareness of her wounded self as it fought back against her abusive yet desperately needed mother. In the following passage, she refers to her anorexia as her way of defeating her mother's constant intrusive comments about her weight. The only difference between Harrison's description of her wounded self and the wounded self in others (like George) is the fact that she was conscious of its existence. Ordinarily, the

wounded self is kept under tight wraps, so tight that the individi
is not aware of its presence:

> I am so angry at her endless nagging me about my weight that I de-
> cide I'll never again give her the opportunity to say a word to me
> about my size. *You want thin?* I remember thinking, *I'll give you
> thin. I'll define thin, not you.* Not the suggested one hundred and
> twenty pounds, but ninety five. And not size six, but size two. If
> only I understood the triumph of refusing to eat; if only I could
> recognize my excitement as that of vengeance, of contriving to
> shut my mother out, the way that she denied me as I stood for
> hours by the bed where she lay, her eyes closed and hidden under
> her mask.   (39)

Harrison lays bare her anger as well as her childhood strategy of
revenge against her mother who wounded her so severely. Her
awareness is far greater now as an adult author who has spent
years in psychotherapy than it was at the time of her anorexia.
Therapy allowed her to identify the excitement she felt as a consequence of her sense of revenge against her mother, both for her intrusiveness and for her neglect. If we took each of her mother's
comments singly they would not appear to have the power to dev-
astate Harrison. Their power came from the fact that her mother
repeated them again and again, with every individual comment
about her weight increasing the anger within her wounded self.
This was particularly true in her history, as she also revealed in her
memoir that her mother offered her almost no compensating experiences of love and support. The continuous criticism was coming
from the very person who should have been supporting and cher-
ishing her. This combination of criticism and lack of love are the
two key ingredients that lead to the development of a wounded self
in many children.

One of my patients, who had been in therapy long enough to
accept and tolerate an awareness of his wounded self, described
the problem of hiding from his anger at his parents as being similar to holding a large beach ball under water. He could do it for

only so long by expending a great deal of energy, but it jumped back up into his awareness the moment a new frustration arose. This is exactly what happened to George at dinnertime: his whole closed computer file of intense feelings popped back onto his screen. He only became aware of these painful realities at dinner; the rest of the time they were completely hidden from his conscious mind.

Novelists also know a great deal about human psychology through intuitive pathways, as the prior quote from Harrison illustrates. Another remarkably wise novelist, Katherine Ann Porter, wrote about the wounded self in her 1948 essay, *The Necessary Enemy*. One of the most important aspects of the wounded self that Porter highlights is the fact that it is so hidden and unknown to the individual that its sudden appearance from its hiding place in the unconscious can be disruptive and frightening:

> She is a frank, charming, fresh-hearted young woman who married for love. She and her husband are one of those gay, good looking young pairs who ornament the modern scene rather more in profusion perhaps than ever before in our history. They intend in all good faith to spend their lives together, to have children and to do well by them and each other—to be happy, in fact, which for them is the whole point of their marriage. . . . But after three years of marriage this very contemporary young woman finds herself facing the oldest and ugliest dilemma of marriage. She is dismayed, horrified, full of guilt and foreboding because she is finding out little by little that she is capable of hating her husband, whom she loves faithfully. She can hate him at times as fiercely and mysteriously, indeed in terribly much the same way, as often she hated her parents, her brothers and sisters, whom she loves, when she was a child. Even then it had seemed to her a kind of black treacherousness in her, her private wickedness that, just the same, gave her her own private life. That was one thing her parents never knew about her, never seemed to suspect. For it was never given a name.
>
> (182–183)

One must admire insights as intuitive and brilliant as Porter displays in this quote. She not only describes the existence of the wounded self, but understands that it develops in childhood and the feelings it contains can be transferred to others. She also recognizes that most of us try to hide from or otherwise deny the existence of the wounded self, and that it paradoxically contains a self-affirming kernel of truth. The truths hidden in the wounded self give the young girl "her own private life." That is, her wounded self knows the truth about past angry and rejecting relationship events within the family, and these mostly hidden perceptions provide her with an authentic perspective. Unfortunately, these truths are encountered in frightening and disruptive ways that tend to make them less credible to the individual. Porter unerringly understood that most individuals experience the emergence of their abused selves with horror and self-disgust. In this passage, the protagonist experiences her wounded self as being traitorous, instead of seeing it as a valuable and accurate source of personal feelings. One of the major steps toward separation from a difficult or neglectful family is to feel comfortable about the contents of the wounded self, without guilt for powerful feelings of anger about events that occurred years ago, and without seeking revenge on those neglectful or abusive family members.

All wounded selves act exactly the same. They remain alive but out of reach, deeply buried in the personality. The wounded self cannot remain repressed forever, as certain events provoke it to burst out of its hiding place and take over the personality. George's wounded self emerged when he was in the presence of an authority figure, either in classrooms with a teacher or when in therapy with me. At other times, with peers, playing hockey, or when alone, it remained a closed file, hidden in his unconscious. The result of a large and active wounded self in adulthood can result in a tremendous outpouring of rage based on a small incident. As a teenager, I was a witness to a sudden upwelling of a wounded self while riding to work with a coworker, a man in his late twenties. One afternoon he stopped on the way home from work at an auto dealership to inquire about trading his car in on a new model. The salesman looked the car over and began negotiating a price. As we drove away, the hood of the car popped partially open, as the salesman had not closed it fully. The young man began swearing and calling the salesman names as he pulled over and closed the hood. Once back in the car he punched the dashboard several times, and threatened to return to the dealership and assault the salesperson. I was one startled and surprised young man—I had no idea what was going on, other than that his reaction was completely out of proportion to the provocation. This experience illustrates what the sudden emergence of a wounded self looks like to an outside observer. The explosive strength of his reaction strongly suggests that this unfortunate man experienced years and years of humiliations during his childhood.

The fury of my coworker's reaction also illustrates another quality of the wounded self, which is its ability to freeze the emotions and perceptions that it contains over long periods of time. The emotions contained in the wounded self are accurate and appropriate feelings experienced at the time of the trauma. Thus, a five-year-old may feel intense humiliation about being punished for wetting his bed, and the intensity of the emotion will remain fresh in his or her memory and will not erode with time. The wounded self is filled with powerful and elemental emotions that can emerge suddenly and with enormous force.

Why Adult Children Allow Their Failed Parents to Dominate Them

Once the wounded self is repressed, the child or young adult can once again relate in a loving way to the parent. The obvious question arises: why does this go on over time? Why can't we remember all the rejecting and negative events in our childhood and accept the fact that our parents failed us, and move on? The answer is deceptively simple. Only psychologically mature young adults can tolerate the reality that their parents failed them in certain areas, because their maturity frees them from needing false but comforting illusions about their parents. That is, their identity is firm enough to allow them to stand on their own without needing the support of their parents. When they no longer need parental support, they also no longer need the defense mechanisms that blinded them (in order to keep them feeling secure) to their parents' failings. Ironically, only adult children of relatively healthy parents (or young adults from less healthy families who have profited from psychotherapy) can see their parent's inevitable failings.

Conversely, young adults who were poorly nurtured cannot tolerate the reality of their parents' failings because they still need their developmental help, as in the case of the toddler who looked at his mother and said "somebody hit me!" The undernurtured young adult simply cannot afford to recognize that the parents he relies on are incapable of offering the support that he desperately needs. This realization would shatter the child's necessary feelings of psychological and emotional attachment to the parent, disrupting the child's hope for the future, and plunging him or her into an abandonment panic. It is often hard to understand why a healthy-looking young adult is so slavishly dependent on his or her parents; however, a look inside their personality would reveal a child with the developmental age of six or seven. The lack of emotional support during their early childhood years traps them in adolescence (or earlier) and they are unable to continue on a normal developmental path. Because they are so desperately needy (and because they repress their active wounded self), they are unable to see that it is futile to hope for love and support from their family in the future. The result of this faulty parenting is large numbers of young adults who are unable to separate from their families. Instead of starting lives of their own, their dependency needs force them to maintain contact with their hostile and negative parents in the hope that someday they will be offered enough emotional support to allow their personality growth to continue.

Harrison is herself an example of a young adult who remained attached to the mother who failed her emotionally. Once again we can observe her uncanny ability to keep track of her wounded self while behaving in ways inconsistent with her real feelings. Like all young adults who were neglected as children, Harrison needed to remain emotionally attached to her mother in the hope that she would eventually receive the love she craved. In the meantime, her pathological mother required that she give up all evidence of self-direction and allowed her (the mother) to take over all decision making:

> After Christmas, my mother and I shop together listlessly. We're going to the same party on New Year's Eve, one hosted by a friend of hers. She's buying me a dress to wear to that party: I'm to choose it with her from the overpriced Laura Ashley boutique. In the store standing under her critical gaze, I am as I was as a child: I command my body to endure the process with as much dignity as possible, while I remain underground, contracted to an unassailable morsel deep within myself, too deep to exhume.
>
> (176–177)

This wonderful description of her inner experience shows us that Harrison was aware of her lack of personal power in the face of her mother's need to control. Despite the fact that she allowed her mother to think that she was completely in charge, Harrison was aware that her true self was deeply hidden and completely immune to her mother's misuse of power. The willful repression of her true self was a conscious technique that preserved her sense of self in the face of her mother's dominance.

Harrison allowed her mother to continue to rule her because she desperately needed her mother, and she needed her mother because (paradoxically) her mother failed her so completely in childhood. Her mother, too, had been so abused by *her* own mother (Harrison's grandmother) that Harrison's mother abandoned her daughter and fled to a secret apartment while Harrison was raised by her grandmother. Harrison had so little contact with her mother that she knew that the only way to continue the relationship was to appear to accept the submissive role without complaint. Her only choice was to submit or to face complete abandonment. Her memoir demonstrates the key paradox that will be examined again and again in this book: children who are not loved and emotionally supported during their critical childhood years face extreme difficulty in separating from their rejecting and abusive parents. All the rejection from her childhood did not discourage her from remaining attached to her mother; instead it made her all the more hungry for her frustrating and elusive parent.

Harrison's example illustrates that neglect has a counterintuitive effect on the development of the human personality. Amazingly, neglect of a child's normal developmental needs makes that child *increasingly attached* to her (faulty) parents as compared to a child who has been reared by nurturing and loving parents. At first glance, this seems to be completely backwards. It seems logical that a child who had very few developmental needs satisfied by her parents would end up being less dependent on others. One might assume that the chronically neglected child would give up the battle to get her developmental needs met and move on in life, but as I have noted, the individual cannot move on without the cooperation of the parent. Thus, no child (or young adult) can give up on her neglectful parents, for to do so assures that her psychological development will stop completely. Similarly, no child stops needing and seeking food if she is being starved. Children simply do not have the emotional fuel to power their own personality development. Thus, the unexpected outcome of childhood neglect is that the child clings to her unloving parent with an intensity and ferocity not seen in the normal child. This is a major part of the explanation of the dynamics of the adult who is unable to leave his or her family of origin. It also is the key psychological factor behind most battered womens' attachments to their physically abusive husbands that I have detailed in *The Illusion of Love*.

This critical developmental reality can be illustrated with the use of numbers. Let us assume that each day in a healthy family results in one unit of emotional nurturance within the child, toward the many thousands of units required for the development of a healthy personality. Thus, a child from a functional, loving family will probably end up with 350 units of nurturance per year. Why not 365 units? Simply because even healthy loving families have some disruptive strife that prevents the child from getting his daily minimum requirement. Thus, each year the loved and emotionally supported child adds 350 units to the required number needed for mature personality functioning. Second, let us assume that it takes 7,000 units of emotional support in total, over a period of twenty years, to allow the child to develop into an adult with a fully mature personality. After ten years of supportive parenting the child has acquired 3,500 units, and after twenty years, 7,000 units, which allows this lucky young adult to achieve emotional maturity. Once achieved, the young adult no longer needs the frequency or intensity of support that was necessary during her development because she carries the thousands of events of emotional support in her memory. She can now separate from her family and eventually begin the process of nurturing the next generation of children.

Now let us compare the healthy scenario with a child caught in an emotionally neglectful family. The lack of support that she experiences allows her to accumulate far too few units of nurturance from her relationships with her parents during the year. Let us assume that she receives seventy-five units out of the 350 she needs, and so she develops a large emotional deficit. Her personality cannot develop normally without these units of emotional support, so it remains stuck at an earlier age. The next year she also receives seventy-five units, so as she gets older, she gets further and further behind in terms of her emotional development. The result of a childhood of continuous deprivation is an enormous deficiency in her identity, and she is left feeling odd and "left behind" as compared to other children her age. Equally damaging is her growing sense of worthlessness, as her wounded self accumulates daily evidence that even her parents do not love her. As time goes on, her damaged identity makes it more difficult—if not impossible—for social service agencies or even kindly relatives to help the deprived child. When outsiders offer her support, it will be reacted to with suspicion, since the child fears being exposed as either needing help or for being the misfit she assumes herself to be. She is therefore cut off from help from school or friends and ever more dependent and fixated on the very parents who are depriving her. As time goes on, she falls further behind in terms of social skills and achievements. As she gets older and her body continues to grow, she is placed in an ever more frightening position with increasing social expectations. Instead of allowing a complex, rich, and confident identity to emerge, she is left with a mostly unconscious wounded self and a childlike, need-driven personality. Many neglected children solve the problem of an incomplete identity by avoiding school functions and outside social relationships, which pushes them deeper and deeper into the web of their neglectful or indifferent family.

As the years go by, her need for a parent (and nurturing in general) will increase, because the previous years of unmet emotional needs are added to the present needs that are not being met. Again, this seems to defy logic, since we generally assume that the older a person is, the less they need the type of emotional support that we offer to children. Worse, the earlier needs are for behaviors that are appropriate at ages four and five, but are no longer appropriate for a young adult. The long-term consequence of emotional deprivation produces a young adult who will try to satisfy his or her unmet childhood needs. Many young people, both men and women, who were developmentally deprived "solve" their personality problem by attaching themselves to a partner who actually represents a parent (even if that partner is equally dependent and immature) and emotionally "weld" themselves to the other person. Often they become pathologically jealous (a reaction to the threat of abandonment) toward potential rivals in their partner's life. These young adults shift their reservoir of unmet childhood needs from their parents to their young partner. Anything that threatens to take this partner away is potentially devastating to their psychological well-being, as they feel that they cannot survive alone. This is the source of most of the jealousy-based violence that takes place in our society.

The neglected child's wounded self is in sharp contrast to the healthy developing sense of self in a child from a functional family who is able to add positive memories to her developing personality on a daily basis. The loved and emotionally supported child has an abundance of memories of affection and feelings of success to add to her ever stronger sense of self. Conversely, the loved child has little or no wounded self, because she has not been exposed to many frustrating and anger-producing events in her relationship to her parents. If a wounded self is not developed in childhood, it will remain undeveloped forever, simply because the child doesn't have to "package" and repress painful events because they never happened. Even when there is conflict in a functional family, the child's chance of humiliation is unlikely because these isolated events are cushioned by the much larger number of loving and supportive interactions that typically take place, as well as the large warehouse of emotionally supportive past events stored in her memory. The consequence of a supportive childhood is a young adult with a strong identity who is not interested in continuing relationships with others who are negative or demeaning. The personality that evolves will be positive and optimistic, unafraid of closeness with others, and based on a foundation of thousands of memories of small successes. This individual no longer needs the support of her parents on a daily, or even weekly basis, as her internalized sense of self becomes her guidance system. Many people mistake healthy individuation from parents as a rejection of the family of origin or lack of closeness. Nothing could be further from the truth. A healthy developmental history allows the individual to separate from his or her family, develop close emotional ties with a partner, and then produce and nurture the next generation. This is impossible for the poorly nurtured individual. They cannot trust others to love them because their own parents failed to do so, or they are consumed with wounded self (as was George), which results in distorted and angry relationships in the next generation.

A Parent Who Was Able to Change

The question that springs immediately to mind is: can the development of a wounded self be reversed once it has begun? The encouraging answer is yes, if the parent reverses their behavior before too much damage has been done to the developing personality of the child. One of my great sources of pleasure in the field of mental health came from working with parents who came in with a "problem" child and were open enough to recognize that they were a major source of the problem. Sadly, this tends to be the exception rather than the rule. Many parents cannot accept that they play any role whatsoever in the difficulty that their child displays. For example, I was consulted by Linda, a thirty-five-year-old graphic artist about her eleven-year-old son. She brought Mark to the session but he refused to come into my consulting room. Rather than engage in a power struggle with the young boy, I suggested that Linda and I talk together while her son remained out in the waiting room, glaring at me with undisguised anger. Linda reported that she was enormously concerned about her son's negativity, hostility, and fascination with violent games on the Internet, particularly in light of the school violence that has captured the nation's attention. She felt that she could not keep her son off the computer, as she had a home office with several modern computers on which she did graphic design. Mark had been given two of her older computers and she did not want to confiscate them, fearing he would continue at a friend's house where she had no ability to supervise him at all.

I began by saying that since her son refused to come in, she and I would have to "cure" him without letting him in on the secret. This seemed to surprise her as she assumed her son was suffering from problems located within himself. Before exploring the problems she was having with Mark, I asked her to describe her own childhood. She immediately challenged me, as she did not see any possibility of a connection between her childhood history and her son's problems. I explained that we often unconsciously bring our own developmental histories into the new family that we create. Linda then willingly described her history which was both emotionally impoverished and filled with verbal abuse from her depressed and bitter mother. She said her goal in life was to raise children who would *never* face what she went through. Her husband was a hard working and dedicated policeman, and they got along well as a couple, but he often worked a second job and consequently he was irritable and tired when he was home. "Well," I noted, "then it's all up to you." Linda was astonished that I had the confidence to predict that she could "cure" her son's problems without her husband's help, and without seeking cooperation from her son—it sounded completely impossible.

I asked her to carry a small notebook in which she drew a line down the center of the page. One side was labeled "rejecting" and the other "loving." I instructed her to rate every sentence she spoke to Mark as either one or the other. We practiced rating typical sentences she might say: for instance, all statements that demanded some activity from Mark without an affectionate tone were rated as rejecting. The very same sentence could move from the rejecting side of the scale to the loving side if it was said in a patient and supportive way. After twenty minutes of practice rating various statements, we both felt that she had understood and mastered the rating task and agreed that we would review her ratings during our second session, scheduled for the following week. Before she left, I emphasized that she was not to change any of her normal behaviors—the only new step was to secretly rate her statements to her son.

I received an emergency call from Linda's husband on the evening of the second day after our initial session. She was locked in her bathroom crying hysterically, saying that she was a worthless parent who was better off dead. He convinced her to talk to me and she immediately (and frantically) described her ratings for the first two days: all of her statements to Mark were on the "rejecting" side of the scale—in two days, she had not made one loving statement. This was a little more reaction than I expected, and so I agreed to meet her later that evening in my office. She showed up escorted by her stunned husband and deeply worried son. Her husband's look seemed to accuse me of driving his wife crazy—after all, she had been perfectly fine until she came into my office just two days ago! Linda's shame prevented her from telling her frightened and confused husband what was going on and thus he had every right to be suspicious of me. I knew I was going to be occupied with Linda for quite a while, and I was worried that all the pained sounds that she was likely to produce would further panic her husband and son, who probably would be able to hear her despite the double doors between my office and the waiting room. So after sitting her down in the consulting room, I strolled back to the waiting room, affected my most casual appearance, and suggested that dad and son go out for a pizza. Linda's husband looked at me as if I were a lunatic—his wife was having a "breakdown" because of my one session with her, and I had the nerve to suggest he take his son out for pizza! I assured them everything would be just fine in two hours or so and they reluctantly left.

Both Linda and I were relieved that she no longer had an anxious family in the waiting room. I began by saying that I thought that I knew what was wrong: she had discovered in the past two days that she had somehow become her mother. "It's true, it's true," she almost wailed (I was very glad that dad and son were not close enough to hear Linda's anguish). This was no wild guess on my part, but rather a simple conclusion based on Linda's description of her mother's behavior toward her, the family dynamic which left Mark with only his mother to rely upon, and Mark's angry and wounded self-withdrawal. Mark's "problem" resulted from having no support from his father and constant criticism from his mother, and thus his only avenue was to withdraw into his own wounded self's fantasies of revenge via the violent games on the Internet. I assumed that Linda was unconsciously enacting the same pattern with her son that she and her mother had engaged in thirty years before.

Linda's two days of rating statements focused her attention on what she was really saying for the first time in her life. After every statement, she would silently rate herself for negativity, in both content and tone. She was amazed that everything she said ended up on the rejecting side of the scale—everything, from getting ready for school to checking Mark's homework. When her son left for school, she sat down and reviewed her ratings, which were depressingly negative. She reassured herself that she was rushed in the morning and would surely have more loving statements in the afternoon when Mark came home from school. To her amazement, the afternoon ratings were even worse than her ratings from the morning. Before bed, she looked at her ratings once again and she reassured herself that the next morning would be better. To her horror the next morning produced more of the same ratings and she spent most of the day stunned by what she had discovered about herself. By the time Linda called me, she was filled with guilt, self-loathing, and despair.

After the shock wore off about my initial remark that she had become her mother, I reassured her that everyone has the potential to turn into their parents, but we could work together and reverse the trend. Linda noted that the worst thing that happened when she began rating her statements was that she remembered how it felt to be abused by her mother. This recognition produced even more pain, as she had broken her vow to never expose her son to the abuse that she felt as a child. Not surprisingly, Linda wanted to change her behavior completely and speak to her son with nothing but loving statements. I knew this was impossible and if she failed (which would surely happen), she would go through yet another bout of intense guilt. Rather than have that happen, I suggested that she continue with her negative statements but add just one loving sentence in the morning and one at night. Linda's mouth dropped open and looked at me as if I was completely out of my mind, saying, "Two a day? That's all I get to say? Two a day?" Now both she and her husband were ready to send me off for treatment of my own!

"Well," I responded, "your son knows that you are coming here," (which was a clear understatement) "and we don't want to make him suspicious that you are saying supportive things just because I told you to. Just say two loving statements to him per day. One before he goes to school, and one when he comes home. That will completely clear up the problem." By the time Linda's husband and son returned, Linda and I were chatting comfortably, and she showed no signs of the deep distress that had overcome her just hours before.

I was confident that Linda was not going to follow our agreement. As expected, she returned the next week with altered scores on her self-rating scale. She had added a new category which she called "neutral," which she used to describe her formerly sharp or cynical statements that she had stripped of their negative tone. Not surprisingly, she had many positive statements, far more than the two per day I had suggested, and had only made a few slips back to the "rejecting" side of the scale. Much to her amazement, Mark was spending less time isolated in his room, so the trend after just one week looked promising. My assumption was that Mark would be very responsive to his mother's improved acceptance of him because his father was absent most of the time. Mark went from being a child of an absent father and a critical mother (equivalent to no parents) to a child with an absent father and a loving mother—a substantial improvement. Linda continued to meet with me regularly for nine months. After she got nearly complete control of her wounded self (that is, when we agreed that she was no longer acting toward Mark as her mother acted toward her as a child), we looked at her painful history with her mother. She was an unusual patient because of her willingness to see parts of herself that many parents simply deny. Happily, the positive trend in her relationship with her son continued and became effortless. This clinical example illustrates my previous point: children's personalities are formed by the small day-to-day interactions with their parents. Both the problem and the cure in this family came in hundreds of small interactions between mother and child.

My work with Linda also demonstrates that many parents do developmental damage to their children inadvertently. Linda was a decent and concerned parent, yet the damage from her own childhood—specifically of the roles that she and her mother were locked into—remained in her unconscious and impelled her to demean her son in the same way that her mother demeaned her as a child. Many children are the innocent victims of their parent's unconscious processes. The vast majority of parents want a good life for their children, yet the hidden power of their wounded self emerges the moment they have children of their own. This happens without warning, because prior to having children, their unconscious had no "actors" to remind them of their childhood role in their original family. However, the moment they have children their unconscious comes alive and begins to re-create their earlier family system, with each of their own children taking on the role of either themselves or a sibling. Thus the child with parents who had difficult childhoods of their own is born into a predetermined interpersonal universe where he or she is gradually defined in the same way that their mother or father unconsciously remembered him- or herself or one of their siblings. Thus, Linda's son reminded her of herself as a child, and she took on her mother's role of constantly criticizing him. This allowed her unconscious wounded self to purge some of the rage it had stored for thirty years, but at a great cost to her son. Fortunately, Linda worked with the insight provided by the rating system and with the motivation from her deep commitment to her son's well-being, which together allowed her to change her behavior. Our work on her own painful childhood relieved much of the unrecognized pain in her abused self, and Mark indirectly confirmed that his mother was an improved parent by his diminished depression, decreased avoidance of family life, and enormous increase in cooperation.

The Development of the Human Identity

The developing child's need for a mother is not just motivated by the need for psychological support, but by the child's need for help in developing a consistent identity. We humans live in a rushing stream of intimate relationships, continuously changing information, social demands, family and business relationships, and relationships to religion, countries, and localities. The bedrock of a mature personality is a fixed sense of self—an identity—that can place us in a realistic and consistent position with respect to this constantly shifting mass of information and relationships. For example, an extremely disturbed individual with a paranoid personality has a distorted identity in that he feels constantly abused and picked upon. He compensates for his feelings of inferiority with fantasies of importance and superiority. If he is pulled over for a traffic stop, his anxiety may overwhelm him and he might believe (because of his defensive grandiosity) that the CIA or the FBI is after him. He may try to flee, or even attack the policeman. His distorted identity has no way of adapting to new information, and he can not tolerate behaving in a submissive manner (that is, accept a relationship that runs counter to his illusions of importance) to an authority figure. Conversely, an individual with a healthy identity knows who he is in relation to a wide variety of circumstances and relationships.

The very beginning of the development of an identity revolves around the infant and his parents, who will hopefully respond to him in a consistent and predictable manner day after day. The child's experience of the world is screened through his parents' perceptions of the universe that surrounds them. Over time, the child finds himself at the same place in relation to the world and this begins to be remembered as a template of reality. The parents' consistent responses allow the child to build up memories of himself and of the world and soon he will feel alive even when his parents are not present. The sense of oneself as existing separately from others is the first step on the road to identity development and it is dependent on the parents' ability and willingness to reflect appropriate and consistent emotionality back to the infant. Chronic neglect and indifference can prevent this very first step in the development of a functional identity in the child, which is defined in the infant or youngster as the ongoing sense that he or she exists when others are not present.

Once again, novelists are often more persuasive than psychologists, and I will return to Kathryn Harrison's memoir *The Kiss* to illustrate how a child experiences the emotional pain of abandonment by a needed parent:

> I make any noise I can that might rouse my mother but that can't be judged as a direct and purposeful assault on the fortress of her sleeping. Because for as long as my mother refuses consciousness of me: I do not exist. As I stand watching her sleep I feel the world open behind me like a chasm. I know I can't step even an inch back from her bed without plummeting. . . . Her eyes, when they turn at last toward me, are like two empty mirrors. I can't find myself in them. (8)

In this passage, Harrison helps us feel how she experienced the abandonment during those times when her mother sought escape from her own rejecting mother's (Harrison's grandmother) oppression by continually sleeping. Once, Harrison purposefully woke her mother and was severely punished, so she learned to wake her mother "inadvertently," just as my patient "George" learned to frustrate his mother by hiding her keys without getting blamed. Harrison, the adult writer, describes how her mother's disinterest in her as a small child damaged her fundamental sense that she existed as a person. It is this need to be recognized, often trivialized as children's need for attention, that supports the early development of a separate and functional identity, and without it the child's sense of herself simply ceases to exist.

Harrison recognized that without her mother's support of her identity she couldn't "step even an inch back from her bed without plummeting." This is a poetic way of saying that without her mother's acknowledgment of her existence, her personality felt like it would disintegrate if she moved away from the source of her security. This is not an exaggeration, but rather the felt experience of all children who are severely neglected. It illustrates the paradox of neglect: the more a child is neglected the greater is her need for the parent. This is one of the two key psychological dynamics that continue to bind adult children to their elderly parents (the other is the illusory hope for future love). The intense dependency that one sees in "adult" children who still live at home is partly a consequence of the lack of a strong identity—an identity that failed to form because of chronic rejection during their development. The individual may be forty years old, yet their sense of self as a separate person who is able to navigate the complexities of the world may be as fragile as Harrison's unformed identity described in the passage.

There is another telling sentence in this quote that Harrison makes her one of the most psychologically astute writers of our time. She recognized that her mother was "blank" when she actually did look at her. This blankness describes her mother's lack of interest in her as a daughter and an inability to validate her

(Harrison's) reactions to the world. We now know from the memoir that this resulted from her mother's experience of being rejected by *her* mother (Harrison's grandmother). Her mother could not give love and nurturing because none was never "put into" her. Emotionally deprived parents cannot love their children because they are themselves "empty" and bereft of emotional attachments. Paradoxically, many have a greedy need to receive love from their children. Harrison had to defend herself from the knowledge that her mother was blank, and assumed that something was wrong with her as a child, rather than recognizing that something was terribly wrong with her mother. This universal false assumption that children make about themselves is called the "moral defense" in Fairbairn's model of human development, and it shifts the blame for being unloved away from the faulty parent to the (innocent) child. It is a defense against reality, because the shift of blame makes the child more secure. It is better to be "morally" defective than to realize that the mother upon whom you are completely dependent is unloving and uninterested in your welfare. This defense will be fully discussed in the next chapter.

The frustrated child does not take neglect lightly, because she needs emotional support and validation from her all-important parent in order to gradually form a new and unique identity. In particular, neglected children become fascinated with and obsess about the missing parent because they need to know who the parent *is* in order to know who they *are*. Often children will seek out their parent's possessions, as they help convey the identity of their parent, which in turn helps them form their own identity. Once again Kathryn Harrison has given us powerful insight into this need, this time in her autobiographical novel *Thicker Than Water*:

> Still, any tangible evidence of my mother, the possessions she had left behind in her bedroom down the hall from mine, the clothes, the china shepherdess on the bookcase, the old satin toe shoes, those cosmetics that were not vital and were left in the cupboard under the bathroom sink—all these things had an ineffable and

weighty presence for me. I handled them in her absence, trying to navigate, by touch and with my unagile, unpracticed young soul, into some understanding of my mother.   (75)

The neglected protagonist in this novel is motivated by her need to discover who her secretive and abandoning mother is in order to form her own identity. The neglected child is at a severe disadvantage as compared to the child with available and responsive parents, she has so little material from her parents to weave into her own developing self. When the need is not met, it does not just evaporate. Instead, the child who cannot identify with the parent often remains at home, enslaved by the unmet need.

The consequence of severe neglect is an incomplete identity, and it leads to the paradoxical observation that many "adult" individuals do not possess fully formed personalities. This statement may be difficult to accept at first glance, since we assume that adult human bodies contain adult human personalities; sadly, such is not the case. The lack of a coherent sense of self is far more common than is generally acknowledged, and there are many chronologically adult humans who have personalities that operate from a childlike perspective. An example that I have used before in *The Illusion of Love* is that of Frieda and Greta, two adult English identical twins who behave in ways appropriate for two young children. The following quote come from an article by John Leo writing for *Time* magazine:

> Greta and Freda Chapin, 37, are identical twins who dress alike, walk in step, take two hour baths together, and frequently talk— and sometimes swear—in unison. If separated, even for a moment, they wail and scream, and when frightened by the taunts of local children, they wet their pants at the same time. The Chapins eat in unison, slowly raising forks and spoons almost simultaneously and finishing up one item on the plate before starting the next. When they argue, they sometimes swat each other lightly with identical handbags, then sit down and sulk together. Many identical twins dress, behave, and think somewhat alike, and even cases

of synchronized speech are not unheard of. But the Chaplins are seen as an extreme example of failure to achieve independent identities.

(45)

These two women demonstrate that it is possible to develop phys ically but remain frozen at an earlier state of personality development. In many ways, their behavior would be acceptable if they were five or six years old. This example also illustrates the previous point, that without a strong attachment to a supportive parent, psychological development ceases. These twins cling to each other the way a child clings to its mother, however, neither could offer the other a mature personality and therefore could not act as a catalyst for development. Therefore they remained tragically stuck at a younger age. The same phenomenon can be observed when young adults with underformed personalities who join cults and fringe groups. These groups attract hordes of "adults" who never had the type of early care that resulted in a solid identity, and they eagerly give up what little personality structure they have and allow the cult to dominate their life.

The Role Played by Our Identity in Everyday Life

An individual's identity consists of a huge computer file of statements about oneself. At the most fundamental level, the first entry says female or male while the second probably states one's age. Other important categories include lovable or unlovable, important or worthless, smart or dull, attractive or unappealing, powerful or ineffectual, and so on. There are thousands and thousands of these statements about the self in each of our identities. What is the "purpose" of an identity? Simply stated, our identity keeps us stable, organized, and functional when we are alone—when there is no one to supply us with feedback as to who we are. Those adults who emerged from faulty families without intact identities have to cling to others in order to keep their personality organized, just like Freda and Greta.

Secondly, and equally importantly, our identity serves as our measuring stick of the universe around us. It acts as a stable point of reference that allows us to define who we are in relation to other people, to the world of work, to our community, and to our families and loved ones. Without a firm identity, we don't know what to believe, where to go, or what to do. Comedy is often based on mistaken identities, concealed identities, or individuals who misunderstand their own identity. For example, the late Peter Sellers played the stupid and bumbling "Inspector Clouseau" in the series of Pink Panther movies. Much of the humor involves the Inspector's complete misunderstanding of his own limitations. He sees himself as brilliant, while in reality he is a fool and a buffoon. His inability to use his identity to locate himself in relation to the capabilities of others is both pathetic and humorous.

In real life, the lack of a firm identity makes everyday tasks an enormous chore. Many patients report that they spend agonizing hours trying to decide "who to be" in various situations. It is extremely anxiety producing to face the world without a steady inner compass and often one family member will prey on others within the family. I have previously used a number of passages from *The Kiss*, a memoir written by Kathryn Harrison. The controversy around this work is based on the fact that she engaged in an incestuous relationship with her father that began when she was twenty years old. She was technically no longer a minor, and therefore her (self-destructive) decision was assumed to be based on her own free will. However, her "free will" was clearly compromised by her deprived childhood which left her with an enormous need to remain attached to her father. Like many adults, her unmet developmental needs overruled both her common sense and her need for self-preservation. The following quotation comes from her father's letters to her:

> Inside my father, his letters confess, are *emptiness, wastelands*, and *black holes* that only my love can fill. *For nearly forty years*, he writes, *I've worked to create the man I've become. What or who lies beneath the surface of all my accomplishments I do not know. You are the only hope of discovering myself.* My eyes move over such words without understanding them. I don't allow myself to hear my

father confess that he lacks identity. He calls as many as three times a day. "How am I?" he says when he calls, and he says this because how he is depends utterly on how much I love him. Without me, there is no meaning, purpose, or pleasure in his life.   (134)

This powerful passage illustrates just how confused and childlike "adults" in dysfunctional families can be. In this instance, Harrison was in the role of parent while her father had regressed to the role of a five-year-old child who needed reassurance every few hours. Neither Harrison nor her father had a functional adult identity, and her father was now trying to use her "love" (which she offered in order to get from him the support that he did not offer when she was an child) to fill in the emptiness and lack of nurturing from his own developmental history. Neither had the ability to "parent" the other, an identical dilemma faced by Freda and Greta, who clung together in a futile attempt to get parenting from each other. Emotional development was not possible for either Harrison or her father in this situation, because both were seeking support for their incomplete identity from an equally incomplete other. Years after the illicit relationship, and after years of psychotherapy, Harrison recognized the impossibility of the situation in this passage, but at the time that she was actively engaged in the incestuous relationship her neediness did not allow to accept the truth.

Her description of her father's dependency on her is reminiscent of a young child's dependency on his mother. Her father's sense of well-being was completely dependent on Harrison's (his daughter's) feelings toward him. His identity was so weak that he could only sustain himself for a few hours before he had to call again for reassurance. Without that reassurance from his daughter "there is no meaning, purpose, or pleasure in his life." This is as clear and as extreme an example of lack of a coherent identity that one can find. The fact that her father regressed back to this earlier stage clearly indicates that his early needs were not met and that his adult appearance concealed an infant-like personality. This example illustrates how vulnerable those with weak identities are to abandonment all through their lives. They live on the very edge of psychological collapse, and not surprisingly, are willing to engage in drastic, antisocial, and self-destructive acts to keep their identities from collapsing.

Helping a Patient with a Weak Identity Separate from Her Needy Parent

I have worked with many patients suffering from underdeveloped identities during my years of practice as a clinical psychologist, one of whom was Terry, an emotionally immature yet optimistic and delightfully humorous individual. She was an unmarried and severely overweight forty-five-year-old businesswoman who owned two wine and cheese specialty shops and loved to say, "Come on Doc, you're the genius, get me outta this mess." She came in for help because her mother would call her several times a day or would suddenly show up at the store and want to talk, thus interfering with her business. Terry had allowed such intrusions in the past, as she had been depressed and underemployed for many years, but recently her first shop had become successful and led to the opening of her second store. They were an important source of her self-worth, and her dependency on her mother decreased drastically. In effect, she was trying to change a longstanding relationship with her mother, which had once met her needs, but now was interfering in her improving life. Her businesses were taking up much of the time she used to devote to her selfish and never satisfied mother. Not surprisingly her mother had few if any friends and was increasing the pressure on Terry to return to their prior pattern of spending almost all of their time in each other's company. The crisis came when the daily intrusions by her mother began to embarrass Terry in front of her customers or suppliers.

Terry's mother was exceedingly self-centered and did not consider Terry a separate individual (which was once an accurate assessment of their relationship). She would call her and without any introductory remarks begin describing an afternoon television program that she was watching. On those occasions that Terry got the courage to hang up the phone her mother would call back and be-rate her for being an unloving daughter. Terry also cleaned her mother's house for her and brought her limitless specialty food items from the store, most of which she rejected because they tast-ed "too ritzy" for her. It was clear that Terry had spent the first half of her life clinging to a mother who had failed her in order to keep her hope of finally being loved alive.

When Terry began to limit her contact because of her business pressures, her mother used a counterstrategy of testing her limits by making ever escalating demands—by being late when Terry went to pick her up and by demanding that Terry drive her around town to do errands because she got "lost" so easily. In utter frustration, Terry bought her a clock with an alarm and a detailed map of the city! Not surprisingly, her mother discarded both of them, com-plaining to Terry that all they did was confuse her further.

Terry's mother was a perfect example of an undeveloped per-sonality lodged in an adult body. Terry described her as behaving like a five-year-old, oblivious to the needs of others, while de-manding that her daughter pay attention to every small detail of her life. Her demanding and childlike behavior illustrates that the hunger for developmental support lives on and on and remains as intense as it was in childhood, despite the fact that the person is now elderly. Terry's mother managed to constantly focus attention on herself, like a child showing off. However, it was too late for that once-critical attention to help her (now) seventy-year-old per-sonality to develop. Her underdeveloped personality still craved at-tention, despite the fact that it was unable to properly utilize the attention as a building block toward normal adulthood. It is simi-lar to a person who was once exposed to near starvation and as a consequence of that experience continually overeats, but the food eaten today has no effect on the memories of past starvation.

Both Terry and her mother suffered from the same type of depri-vation (like Harrison and her father). The only difference was that they were in different roles based on their generation and relation-ship. It is easy to assume that Terry's elderly and self-centered mother failed to meet even a fraction of her legitimate developmental needs, leaving her in a state of psychological suspended animation. She still clung to her mother in the hope that she would somehow get her mother's support in order to make up for all the years during which her needs were not met. Terry's dependency allowed her mother to use her child-like attachment to her own advantage. Terry's extreme need also blinded her to the fact that her mother did not have the love within herself to give to others.

When I am faced with an "adult" patient who is demonstrates high levels of dependency and poor separation on a previously neg-lectful parent, I know that every suggestion I make for independent action will be seen as impossible, cruel, or excessive. Thus, I knew better than to suggest that Terry set limits on her mother since it was clear that her mother acted as half of her identity. Rather, I suggested that she meet with me twice a week. This had the effect of further compressing Terry's time with her mother and it placed me "inside" their previously exclusive two-person world. I also knew that the emotional attachment that Terry would develop to-ward me would threaten her mother, which was indeed the case. During our third or fourth session my phone, which has an auto-matic answering machine, began ringing time after time. Terry sheepishly admitted that her mother planned to call her during the session and demand to speak to me. I simply got up and pulled the phone jack out of the wall. "Don't do that!" Terry yelled. "My mother will kill you!" I looked down at my lap in stony silence and then in a deep and growling voice responded, "I eat people like your mother for breakfast!" Terry stared at me in wild-eyed aston-ishment, amazed that I could be so bold an unafraid of her seem-ingly all-powerful mother. She then said with mock horror, "Oh, you're one of them tough guys I'm supposed to steer clear of— aren't you, Doc?" "Yep, that's me," I said. "Your old mom doesn't scare me a bit."

Our light and humorous approach did not change my assess-ment of Terry as a child trapped in an adult's body, and we spent many hours discussing small tasks that intimidated her, including developing her network of friendships, continuing her education, and the most frightening task of all: entering the world of dating.

Her mother continued to remind both of us of her anger at being displaced—once she parked right next to my first-floor office and ran her car engine throughout the session to remind us of her presence and displeasure at Terry's growing independence. After six months of sessions, Terry told her mother she could no longer barge into her stores during business hours and interfere with her customers. Her mother had seen the progress Terry was making, and agreed to this condition without any retaliation, as she recognized that her power over Terry was waning. Over the next three years, Terry gradually won the battle against her mother's intrusiveness. For the first time in her life, she developed a healthier identity that could stand up on its own and develop a network of friendships that became the focus of her life experience.

TWO

How Our Defenses Play
"Hide and Seek" with Reality

Nostalgia runs deep in the human psyche . . . it converts healthy
dissatisfactions into an atavistic longing for a simpler condition,
for a childhood of innocence and happiness remembered in all
its crystalline purity precisely because it never existed.

—*Peter Gay*

This chapter continues the discussion of childhood dependency. It
is simply impossible for us to remember just how desperately dependent we were as children, but one common scene will bring this
universal human reality back into focus. I was shopping in a large
store recently when I heard the distinctive wail of a toddler who
had lost sight of his mother. I peeked around the corner of the aisle,
and there he was—an enormously distressed two- or three-year-old
little fellow yelling his heart out. Not surprisingly, several adults
had come to his aid, but they seemed to make him wail even loud-
er, as they were clearly *not his mother*. Finally, a harried looking
woman with two other young children turned the corner and called
"Tom-my!" The effect of her voice was electric; he snapped around
and the moment he caught sight of her he stopped crying. Suddenly his world was complete and safe and he trotted toward her as
fast as he could. No other adult in the entire store, no matter how
skilled at parenting, had the power to relieve him of his panic except his all-important mother. We forget that each and every one of
us was once as dependent as this little boy. Those of us (including

myself and nearly all my adult friends) that were either neglected or abused in our childhoods had to find techniques to remain emotionally and psychologically attached to our parents despite the inadvertent rejection of our emotional needs.

Neglect and abuse are two different but closely related factors, both of which can delay development. Neglect can occur independently or it can occur as a by-product of abuse. When a child is abused, he is suffering from two damaging developmental events occurring at the same time. Returning to the example of the family dynamic between George and his mother, we see that during the time that George and his sister were being forced to eat (abuse), they were also being deprived of the support and emotional nurturing (neglect) that they should have been receiving at the dinner table. When George shifted into his wounded self at the dinner table, he was not only filled with anger and humiliation, but also felt extremely alone because his bond to his mother was broken. He had suddenly lost the single person in the universe upon whom he depended to make himself feel safe, secure, and wanted. He faced a critical and unsolvable conflict: he needed a close relationship with his mother in order to feel safe and secure during the day, yet his mother humiliated him at the dinner table each night. His intense anger was incompatible with seeing his mother as a supportive anchor in the uncertain sea of childhood. Thus, each dinner she was lost to him in terms of making him feel secure.

George was both abused and neglected at the dinner table. Other children are less abused than he was, but are neglected almost continuously. Neglect sounds less damaging than abuse—however, that is not always the case. Children do not experience neglect as a neutral void. Instead, neglect produces a state of need and intense longing for the emotionally missing parent. This has enormous consequences in the future development of their personality. Neglecting a child is like starving it: the longer the child goes without food, the more the child focuses on his hunger, and the more he tries to meet his needs with fantasy. The very presence of a parent who neglects a child is like showing a starving child a banquet that is sealed off by a glass wall. The food tantalizes the child to the point of distraction, as does the parent who refuses to nurture his or her desperately needy offspring.

Children in disorganized families cannot change their parents; their only option is to develop psychological defense mechanisms that keep them from becoming too anxious about the reality in which they are forced to live. George, along with all abused and neglected children, had to discover a way to psychologically reinstate his mother in his own mind as a loving parent. Part of the solution is for the child to isolate the worst memories of neglect in their wounded self and repress it in the unconscious. That process removes the relationship's destructive anger and hurt. A second process restores hope for the child to hold onto when the reality of the family provides too little support. This second part of the defense mechanism allows the child to redeem his parent by creating the illusion that his mother (or father) will improve in the future. This comforting illusion becomes a counterweight to the mostly unconscious wounded self and it is present in all abused and neglected children to keep them from experiencing intense depression and outright psychological collapse. This second part of the same defense is called the "hopeful self." The hopeful self that George created was an illusory belief that his mother was a good parent who would eventually support his need for autonomy and show him more affection in the future. He created this illusion by exaggerating and amplifying the rare but actual memories of support from his mother that he could recall, which involved his success as a hockey player. Every child's continuous need for emotional support demands that he retain hope for the future, and his unmet developmental needs are the motivation for the creation of an elaborate and powerful illusion that his parents are better than they really are. The hopeful self becomes an alternative and less troubling view of his mother's "reality" than is contained in his (mostly unconscious) wounded self. The illusion that every child creates is that his parents have the potential to love him, which allows him to feel love for himself. The hopeful self serves as a lifesaving antidote to the bitter and envious wounded self, which often becomes committed to destroying the rejecting aspects of the parents or other adults in positions of authority.

The hopeful self's misperception of the mother or father is the reciprocal "partner" to the wounded self, and together they operate as the two halves of the primary defense mechanism of childhood. The hopeful self defends the child from confronting the intolerable reality that there is little actual hope for love or support from his parent(s), and the wounded self keeps the memories of pain and despair tightly bottled up in the unconscious.

An excellent example of the development of a hopeful self in a well-known person can be seen in Doris Kearns Goodwin's biography of Eleanor Roosevelt, *No Ordinary Time*. A typical example of parental failure suffered by Eleanor occurred when she and her charming but alcoholic father were walking together with their three dogs in New York City and passed the Knickerbocker club. Her father entered and told her that he would be out in a few minutes. Eleanor was left waiting by this well-meaning but immature and self-centered parent with the dogs for five hours and when he reappeared he was so drunk that he had to be carried home. Her father loved her when he was sober, but he bitterly disappointed her when he was drinking. These extreme and opposite experiences furnished her hopeful self with the illusion that she was loved, and simultaneously her wounded self was filling with memories of repeated and intense disappointments. Eleanor hid from the memories of her father's parental failures in her repressed wounded self, while memories of his charm and endless promises of love were in her awareness, in her hopeful self.

Her relationship with her father was of primary importance to her and had to be preserved, because her mother was almost entirely rejecting. In fact, her beautiful mother seemed repelled by young Eleanor's plainness, and humiliated her with the nickname "Granny." By the time Eleanor was seven, her father was living away at sanatoriums for treatment of his alcoholism and she was satisfying her need for a loving parent by creating a hopeful self based on his romantic letters to her:

> On her eighth birthday, Eleanor received a long and loving letter
> from Abingdon (the sanatorium where her father was hospitalized),

addressed to "My darling little Daughter." He wrote, "Because father is not with you is not because he doesn't love you . . . For I
love you so tenderly and dearly. And maybe soon I'll come back all
well and strong and we will have such good times together, like we
used to have."   (93–94)

These letters, filled with only love for her, Eleanor later wrote, were
the letters she loved and kissed before she went to bed.

Luckily, Eleanor had powerful defense mechanisms well established by the time she faced three major losses. One month after her
eighth birthday her mother, her only available parent, died. She was
then sent to live with her grandmother while her father remained in
treatment for alcoholism. The following year, her four-year-old
brother died, and soon after, so did her beloved father:

"My aunts told me," Eleanor recalled, "but I simply refused to believe it, and when I wept long . . . I finally went to sleep and began
the next day living in my dream world as usual. From that time on
. . . I lived with him more closely, probably, than when he was
alive.   (95)

Eleanor was faced with a series of traumatic emotional abandonings from the time of her birth that required the development
of powerful defense mechanisms to keep her from psychological
collapse. Her attachment to her father was much stronger than to
her mother, both because her father's larger-than-life promises
served as fuel for her hopeful self and because her mother offered
her so few moments of love upon which to build her hopeful self's
fantasy. She took her mother's death in stride because by that time
all of her attachment needs were focused on her father, whom she
assumed would return home after treatment. Even when he did not,
her hopeful self maintained her psychological stability throughout
her childhood by immersing her in a dream world that was filled
with the illusion of love.

All children from dysfunctional families, rich or poor, rely on
the hopeful self as a defense against the collapse of their entire

personality. I recently worked with a bright thirty-year-old woman who arrived at her regular psychotherapy session with a small ceramic angel that had been given to her by her father on her tenth birthday. It was obvious that she treasured this powerful symbol of love; it was the only gift her father had ever given her and it became the cornerstone upon which her hopeful self was built. She would not allow me to touch it for fear that I might harm the precious memento. She began to cry as she described the morning on which she found the gift at her place on the dining room table. Her father's token was exceedingly important, as her mother was physically abusive and treated her like a second-class citizen.

I was soon to learn however, that there was a second, painful reality about her father that she described to me months later in our therapy sessions. It was eerily absent from her awareness while she showed me the small angel. The unavailable reality about her father was repressed in her wounded self, and it was completely hidden during the sessions when her hopeful self was dominant. This separate reality about her father was that he ignored her completely during her early childhood, and worse, his behavior changed dramatically when she matured into a sexually appealing young woman, at which point he suddenly became attentive. On several occasions, when her mother was out visiting friends, he made overt sexual advances toward her. She was enormously frightened by this turn of events, and she began to avoid her father whenever possible. The moment she became a teenager, her rebellious wounded self emerged, and she became pregnant by a boyfriend. Upon learning of her pregnancy, her father forced her to leave the family home and live in a rooming house because she had disgraced the "family name." To this selfish man, his daughter's welfare was less important to him than his own sexual needs, or later, than the opinion of his relatives and neighbors. None of these painful and anger-provoking memories were present when my patient showed me the little angel, as all of her negative memories about him were hidden away in her wounded self, deeply repressed in her unconscious. These painful memories of betrayal were isolated and ignored when her naive and optimistic hopeful self was dominating her sense of reality.

In adulthood, our need for the fantasy of loving parents does not disappear. Most adults are compelled to continue to hold on to the illusions that they were loved as children, because a clear view of the harsh childhood realities would cause an upwelling of grief and anger so powerful that it would seriously disrupt their lives. My patient's hopeful self's fantasy was constantly challenged by the memories stored in her wounded self. These two opposite views had to be kept apart or her fragile equilibrium would disintegrate. Like Eleanor Roosevelt, my patient focused most of her attachment needs on her father, and despite the fact that she was an "adult," she still felt too needy to tolerate the possible loss of the fantasy that her now deceased father once loved her.

If the "adult" of thirty finds it difficult to face this reality, imagine how absolutely impossible it is for the child of ten! The daily support of parents is crucial to all children's ability to continue functioning, so they create illusions as large as necessary to keep themselves going. This is the reason behind the paradoxical observation that the least loved and emotionally supported children have the most elaborate and unrealistic fantasies about their parents. These extreme hopeful selves have to be unrealistic, as they keep the hope of love alive in the child when there is little or no real love or support within the family. When a child is dominated by her hopeful self, she will refuse to believe that her parents are not interested in her plight—information that is equivalent to telling a parachute jumper that her chute is all tangled up, but she must jump anyway. The anxiety from this knowledge is simply too much to bear.

Once established, the hopeful self can destroy a young adult's attempt to separate from his or her dysfunctional family. The following example, which I have used previously in my book *The Treatment of the Borderline Personality*, illustrates how destructive the hopeful self can be to the individual trying to separate from a destructive family:

Pam, a beautiful young woman of twenty-five, came for therapy because of her struggles with her family. Her father was a successful homebuilder who employed her two brothers, but Pam had been completely ignored by him both in childhood and now in her young adulthood. As part of our work, Pam spent several months getting up the courage to leave her unhappy family and successfully saved money from her salary as a secretary for a deposit on an apartment. To her amazement, the moment she moved out of the family home, her father called and begged her to return. Pam was utterly confused and conflicted by her father's behavior because he had been completely indifferent toward her when she lived at home. Her wounded self (which was no longer repressed and was the focus of our discussions in therapy) was filled with clear memories of her father's rejection of her legitimate needs as a daughter. His surprising new behavior did not match her well-established views. He not only called her, but sent a completely uncharacteristic emotional card "To My Loving Daughter" in which he professed a deep parental love for her. This was puzzling because Pam and her mother were treated like servants by her father and two brothers. Their job was to do all of the housework and prepare the evening meal and lunches for the next workday while remaining otherwise invisible. Pam noted that her father would not even respond to her when he was engaged in conversation with either of her two brothers. Pam's mother self-destructively solved her problem of an insensitive and neglectful husband by drinking to the point of passing out almost nightly. One of Pam's unspoken jobs was to take her comatose mother upstairs and put her to bed.

Despite our work, Pam's unmet childhood needs had created a hopeful self that was stimulated by her father's craftily aimed card and calls. She was unable to resist the promise of love that her father offered in his card, and her previously dominant wounded self's view of him was repressed and replaced with her hopeful self's view of him, one that was unaware of all the childhood rejection. Predictably, after one month of living alone in her new apartment, the promise of love coupled with the loneliness she felt without familiar (albeit unloving) family members around her convinced her to move back in with her family. There was absolutely nothing that I could say that would change her mind. Her mother was overjoyed and her father seemed more responsive to her than before. Pam terminated treatment with me, thinking her problems with her family were solved. About two months later she returned, saying that her father was no longer paying any attention to her and her mother was more of a burden than ever. Pam's hopeful self, which seemed so powerful just weeks before, could not stand up to the reality of daily rejections once she resumed her role as family servant. Over time it gave way and was replaced by her wounded self once again. Once her wounded self again became the dominant reality she could remember how indifferent her father had been all during her development. With my support and encouragement, she began saving for another rent deposit and soon after moved out for the second time. I prepared Pam for her father's now predictable manipulation, saying that she should expect another plea to return home. Within a week of her move, another flowery card arrived from her father. The struggle between her hopeful self and her wounded self was reactivated by the card, and despite my best efforts, her need-driven hopeful self won out again. She saw her father as filled with potential love, while her more accurate view of him as a manipulator and user were repressed in her once again unconscious wounded self. She gave up her apartment, moved back in with her family, and the cycle began all over again.

This example shows just how extreme and unrealistic decisions made by the hopeful self can be when it is dominant. Pam's unmet childhood needs were not apparent when she was dominated by her wounded self, but her repressed hopeful self emerged powerfully when she was faced by the seductive promises of love offered by her father. Pam's faulty choice was based on fantasy and need, not on reality—she fell in love with her own self-created illusions.

A number of readers have used the word "addiction" to explain Pam's attachment to her father. Her hopeful self acted like a drug, blinding her to the reality of her father's indifference—an indifference that she was only able to access while in therapy. "Addiction" is an overused and superficial description that is assumed to be an explanation, when in fact, it is simply an observation. The description of Pam as an "addict" tells us nothing about her underlying psychological dynamics, and it gives no hint of the role of her hopeful self nor of the unmet developmental needs that motivate this form of self-destructive defense mechanism. It does not begin to help us understand the processes that motivate this extremely odd and self-defeating attachment, and it creates the false impression that we have an explanation when in fact all we have is a surface description.

The Splitting Defense

The complex defense mechanism that keeps the hopeful self and the wounded self unaware of each other, even though they coexist in the same person, is called the "splitting defense" or simply "splitting." It allows the child (and later, the adult) to see others only in terms of the two opposite and isolated viewpoints. Persons who use the splitting defense can suddenly shift their view of the parent (or significant other) from their hopeful self's perspective to their wounded self's perspective (or vice versa) in a matter of seconds. In effect, the dependent and emotionally starved child has managed to psychologically separate his depriving but needed mother or father into two distinct and separate people; a anger-inspiring rejecting parent and a emotionally-longed-for loving parent. The splitting defense actively keeps the two opposite views of the parent apart in their minds. Neither my patient Pam nor young Eleanor Roosevelt could afford to allow the memories of neglect in their wounded selves to confront the unrealistic fantasies in their hopeful selves. If their wounded self memories of their fathers' behavior met and confronted the opposite hopeful self fantasy, the wounded self memories would overwhelm and destroy the "good" fantasy father that they created. Wounded self-memories are "real" memories— the events stored in the wounded self actually happened—while hopeful self fantasies are illusions based on the child's pressing hopes and dreams. The splitting defense protects the two opposite selves from meeting, thus saving the unrealistic optimism of the hopeful self from being destroyed by the wounded self. In Pam's case, her wounded self knew that her father ignored her, was willing to use her as a servant, and was not truly interested in nurturing

her. If this reality forcibly confronted her hopeful sel
ed self memories would destroy the hopeful self fant;
reality was exposed, it could plunge Pam into an ;
panic, a condition akin to the terror experienced by
in a supermarket.

The splitting defense is neither a "split personality" nor a "multiple personality." The concept of a split personality came from
early work with schizophrenic patients who "split" their emotions
from their verbal productions. Thus, a schizophrenic might describe a sad event while giggling. This concept has been largely
dropped from mental health, though it does live on in fiction and
film. A multiple personality is a rare and very serious disorder
which usually results from extreme abuse in childhood. The child
must develop separate selves to tolerate different feelings. Each of
the subpersonalities that are developed are distinct and often do
not know about the others, but each is a functional and relatively
complete personality. A patient with multiple personality disorder
may wake up in a strange place, or with odd clothing on (that
"belongs" to one of the other personalities) and not know what
happened. In contrast to the rare multiple personality disorder,
the splitting defense is very common and the same personality in-
habits each self—the difference is the perspective or view of others currently held. The hopeful self view of the parents is rosy and
unrealistic, while the wounded self's view is negative and filled
with pain.

The splitting defense is not a new way of thinking and feeling,
but rather an earlier form of emotionality that failed to mature. We
are all familiar with the toddler who suddenly shifts in emotion
from saying "Mommy, I love you" to "Mommy, I hate you." These
fast fluctuations in emotion occur in very young children because
they cannot hold on to past images of the mother as a loving person when they are frustrated. Thus when frustration occurs, the
toddler—who is perpetually caught in the moment—cannot recall
the events of two minutes ago, when her mother was responding as
loving parent. Her emotions can and do swing from love to anger
in a second. This style of immature emotionality remains alive in

unloved children throughout their lives because the mountain of painful memories contained in their wounded selves would destroy their attachment to the needed parent. Thus, the purpose of splitting is to keep the child or undernourished adult from psychological collapse by hiding the reality that he or she was not really loved or cared for as a child. As long as the illusion of a loving family persists, the individual will be able to function in life.

This defense is resistant to pressure from others, including interpretations from the "helpful" therapist. If, for instance, I insisted on reminding my patient whose father made a sexual approach toward her of this (now repressed) fact when she was dominated by her hopeful self, she would be (genuinely) offended and feel that I did not understand her at all. I would be both wasting my time and alienating my patient. The "reality" that her father tried to seduce her is so completely repressed by the splitting defense that no memory trace is available to her. Her hopeful self, when dominant, only has access to those perceptions and illusions that indicate her father loved her; it is the only "truth" that makes any sense to her.

There is a great personal cost to the individual who uses this defense. It can, as with Pam, sabotage a young adult's attempt to separate from his or her unloving family. Second, behaviors the individual cannot control that emerge from the repressed wounded self can ruin the patient's reputation. If we return to George, the prep school student who stole items from my office, it was clear in our sessions that the hostility in his wounded self, which was filled with memories of his combative relationship with his abusive mother, were being reenacted by him in his self-destructive game-playing with authority figures. During our sessions, George continued to view his childhood through the illusion of his hopeful self and thus his revenge-driven stealing both from the school faculty and from my office seemed to emerge from outer space.

As we have seen, the result of a childhood filled with deprivation is the development of two separate selves and the splitting mechanism which keeps them apart. The consequences of the splitting defense is a deep loyalty to our failed parents that is difficult to break. Thus Fairbairn's concept of "attachment to bad objects" is fueled by both sides of the splitting defense. The "love," or more accurately, the "need-driven" side of the attachment is the realm of the hopeful self, which varies in intensity from person to person. The second part of the attachment to failed parents flows through the angry and vengeful wounded self. Each wounded self is unique, because different childhood experiences of either neglect or abuse produce different intensities of memories of anger and despair. The wounded self does not want to give up on the neglectful parent, because the child knows that it cannot exchange its parents for better ones. This emotionally charged focus on the parent does not change once adulthood is reached. Rather, the wounded self first tries to reform the parent and turn him or her into a loving parent. After years of disappointment, some children give up their hopeful self fantasies, and instead focus on the memories in their wounded selves. They remain attached to their parents through the desire to punish or expose the parent to public scrutiny, much like "whistle-blowers" who spend their lives exposing corruption in corporations or in government. The wounded self is as intensely attached to the rejecting parent as the hopeful self is to the illusory loving parent. It has no interest in separating from the rejecting parent any more than a deprived child of eight or nine is interested in leaving its family.

It is preferable to use the word "attachment" rather than "love" in the explanation of futile relationships to failed parents. These two words are easily confused and are both burdened with other meanings that can muddy the issue. When we use the word "attachment," we usually mean it in positive terms. However, all neglected children remain attached to their parents despite the fact that there was very little love present during their developmental years. Emotional attachments forged under conditions of deprivation are based on a reservoir of unmet developmental needs and these attachments are not healthy, but they are very strong—even desperate—attachments nonetheless. As I have demonstrated, need-based attachments become increasingly powerful over time because the unmet needs never stop demanding satisfaction.

Blaming Ourselves for Imaginary Failures

Fairbairn also describes a second and far less complex defense mechanism than the splitting defense. This defense is commonly used by children and is called the "moral defense." Simply stated, the child blames himself or herself for imaginary faults and these imagined failures justify their parents' punishments or indifference. This defense mechanism preserves the child's attachment to his parents by placing the blame for being rejected directly on his or her shoulders. Unlike the automatic actions of the splitting defense, the moral defense is based on logic (faulty logic, but logic nonetheless) and is a conscious attempt by the child to make sense of his unfortunate lot in life.

How does a seven-year-old child accomplish this psychologically significant task? It is actually quite simple: all she has to do is blame herself for *causing* her parent's neglectful or abusive behavior. If she is morally at fault, then her parents' behavior is transformed into a reasonable reaction to her badness. That is, if the child convinces herself that she is deserving of punishment for being dirty, slow to get ready, stupid, or sassy, then she has created a reason for her parent's behavior—behavior that in reality is inexcusable. This self-blame gets the parents "off the hook" as being bad parents, and this allows the young needy child to remain attached to her reinvented "good" parents without experiencing overwhelming levels of anxiety.

The reverse is simply impossible. If a seven-year-old child were able to clearly understand that her parent's rejection, abuse, or neglect of her came from their indifference or out of pure meanness, then she could no longer remain securely bonded to them and would disintegrate with anxiety. Nothing is more terrifying than being hopelessly dependent on someone who either wants to hurt you or is indifferent to your needs. Thus, all children blame themselves for causing their parents' neglect of them which effectively shifts the burden of blame to the already vulnerable self of the child.

The moral defense emerges as the child grows older, after both the development of language and after the awareness that she is being excessively punished emerges. She must develop an excuse for her parent's rejecting behavior because no child of seven, eight, or nine can consciously accept that her parents are either malicious or indifferent to her needs. Let us not forget that children with unloving parents have no other choices available to them—they can neither find new parents, nor force the parents they have to love them. Worse, the chronically deprived child is in a worse "bargaining" position than the well-supported child because her impoverished emotional history has left her with a reservoir of unmet developmental needs that cry out for satisfaction. These pressing needs force her to focus intense hope on her parents—the very parents who have failed her. Conversely, the well-supported child can rely on her own memories of her past successes. They form the foundation of her developing personality, and allow her to stand up for herself because, paradoxically, she is not as dependent on her parents.

The moral defense is a conscious defense and the child accuses herself of having one or more moral failures, while simultaneously making logical excuses for the parent's rejecting behavior. Once again I will use the insights of Kathryn Harrison to demonstrate how the moral defense can be used to recast and minimize the shortcomings of parents, this time from her novel *Thicker than Water*:

> To myself, aloud, I might say, "My mother was an unfulfilled person and unhappy." Or, "Mother always regretted that she didn't pursue her ballet." Or the more dangerous, "Mother loved me, she just wasn't ready to have a child. It wasn't that she didn't love me, she was just young and selfish. It was because I reminded her of my father that she was sometimes unkind . . . "   (88)

This poignant passage illustrates the endless struggle of the child to keep the parents "good" by making herself "bad." The protagonist in the novel excuses and minimizes her mother's rejecting behavior and then blames herself for reminding her mother of the husband that she hated. She tries to convince herself that she has a good mother, even though the reality was quite the opposite. If she did not succeed in this psychological transformation, she would face complete abandonment. The moral defense allows the child to give the parents an excuse for their inexcusable behavior, because the loss of the illusionary relationship with them (if the truth were finally accepted) would be devastating.

The following example is of a long-term patient of mine who took years to get over his defense of blaming himself for his parents' abuse.

Richard was the oldest of three sons of a middle-class industrial engineer and schoolteacher. His family had all the trappings of suburban normalcy, yet he felt deeply alienated from them. His father, himself the son of an abusive stonemason, found fault with nearly everything Richard did. Like most parents, his father disguised his maltreatment of his son with the rationalization that he was helping Richard to become a better student. In truth, he was reenacting the same abusive relationship that he had endured with his own father, translating the physical brutality of his own childhood into intellectual and emotional brutality. It was likely that Richard's father had forgotten the details of his own painful history, but his wounded self now found a victim on which to discharge the accumulated rage from his own childhood. At dinner, Richard was asked to report on what he had learned at school that day, and his father would then make up questions about that topic and quiz his son. For instance, if the topic was world history, his father would ask how many countries Alexander the Great had conquered. Richard was almost always unable to answer his father's impossible and hostile questions and as a consequence he was forced to leave the table, and could only return after he had looked up the answer. His father, like many autocratic parents, coerced the rest of the family into applauding his teaching "program." Naturally, the family's acceptance of this procedure confused Richard, and he felt tortured and rejected. He couldn't reconcile his angry, self-hating feelings with the family approval of his father's methods. Over time, Richard protected his attachment to his father by using the moral defense: he considered himself to be mentally retarded, which justified the harsh treatment that he was accorded. He speculated that he had been mistakenly placed into his highly successful family, but was in fact a foreigner. He based this conclusion from reading articles in National Geographic that contained pictures of primitive peoples from New Guinea. He thought that he had a similar facial structure to one particular tribe, and thus concluded that was why he was finding his father's questions so difficult. He believed that he had been switched in the hospital, and thus he deserved to be humiliated.

When Richard told me of his conclusion about his genetic heritage I was confronted by the moral defense at its strongest. He was absolutely convinced that he had been switched in the hospital, and that explained why he had what he considered his limited intellectual capacity. His elaborate and creative use of this defense completely exonerated his father for being cruel and abusive toward him, and conversely, it labeled him as retarded. He dismissed the contradictory reality of his high scores on his college entrance exams by saying that the testing company had made a mistake. Not surprisingly, his father (who was unaware of how abusive he had been), took credit for Richard's high entrance exam scores, noting how successful his educational program had been. Richard's father's poorly controlled wounded self, which acted out sadistically toward him, was never openly acknowledged and thus both father and son were prevented from seeing how badly the father had undermined his son's sense of self.

Predictably, Richard's impoverished developmental history came back to haunt the entire family. During his first semester at college he experienced a complete emotional collapse as he did not have enough of an identity or internal strength to allow him to separate from his abusive (but still needed) parents or to face the demands of school. He returned home a failure and took a number of menial jobs, but his wounded self was so sensitive to criticism and actively rebellious toward his supervisors that he was frequently fired. This is a very common pattern with many dependent and angry young men as they direct the full force of the anger in their wounded selves toward "safe" authority figures on whom they can vent their frustration. An employer or boss is safer than the parent because getting fired does not endanger the tie to the family. More concretely, there was no chance that Richard would be asked to leave his home, because he was fired from his job as a meter-reader for the public utility company—a position his family considered beneath him in the first place. At home, Richard's unmet dependency needs and resentment allowed him to take money from his parents long after he should have been supporting himself. He also took perverse satisfaction in social situations when he was regarded as a family embarrassment by his prominent parents, who made up false stories about his success. In our work together, it took Richard a year before he let go of the fantasy of his parent's "goodness," which was the cornerstone of his defensive attachment to them.

The moral defense works in parallel with the splitting defense to keep the child, and later the young adult, attached to parents who have continually failed to meet his or her emotional and developmental needs. The most unfortunate result of this defense is the destruction of the child's, and later the young adult's, confidence in him- or herself. Many children who use the moral defense get so used to taking the blame that they become easy targets for emotional exploitation when they finally get out into the world.

The Complex Issue of Responsibility

Unhealthy attachments can either remain focused on the original parents or they can be shifted outside of the family. When a child from a unloving family does manage to separate, his very first choice of a romantic partner will be the new focus of all of his unmet hopeful self-needs as well as his repressed wounded self-anger. One of the most common scenarios in late adolescence occurs when a neglected son or daughter, one who is unconsciously driven by these two isolated selves, brings a spectacularly unsuitable future partner home and announces that he or she is in love. I have been consulted by many anguished parents who seek help in convincing their son or daughter not to marry a partner who they see is clearly unsuitable. For example, I was consulted by a major developer in my area about his daughter who was a recent gradu- ate of our local community college. She had begun a job as an as- sistant to a telephone sales company and decided to marry the star salesman, a man with a checkered personal history and career. His success consisted of badgering phone customers into opening ac- counts with a credit card company—and he was very good at this task. Her future husband had overcome drug addiction and had also admitted to being a past abuser of women, two characteristics which horrified her prominent and successful parents.

I began interviewing the various members of this family, and it became clear that the daughter had unconsciously chosen this par- ticular man as her future partner because he allowed her to act out all the intense feelings contained in both of her hidden selves. Her childhood consisted of an endless merry-go-round of caretakers that were needed because the demanding professional life of her fa- ther and equally pressing social life of her mother left no time for them to care for her. When I interviewed her and asked her about the past difficulties of her future husband I was provided with her pure hopeful self's view of him. She simply could not see her future husband's negative characteristics consciously. However, with little prompting, the privacy of our sessions together allowed her wounded self to emerge and she clearly described the constant frus trations and endless abandonings of her childhood. She also noted, without seeming to make the connection, that her intended hus- band was quite self-centered and often ignored her completely. My interviews with her strongly suggested that her wounded self had played an equal role with her more available hopeful self in her decision-making process. Her wounded self recognized (uncon- sciously) that her new partner would be a powerful opponent: a man who would withhold love, one who she could attempt to re- form, and one who would be a constant source of frustration that would allow her wounded self to pour out its ancient anger from childhood. In short, her wounded self recognized that this young man promised to be as impossible as her parents! He also served as a conscious vehicle for revenge against the rejecting aspects of her parents, who had neglected her throughout her childhood but who were now finally paying attention to her. When they condemned her future husband directly, she defended him ferociously and bonded to him more tightly, thus defeating the power that her parents once wielded.

Children from unloving families try to keep their wounded self repressed and therefore their hopeful self is the conscious part of their personalities most of the time. The parents of the young woman were faced with a daughter who could only see the potential for love and romance with this flamboyant and self-inflated young man. Her parents, who were not using the splitting defense, were able to see the total personality of the young man that their daughter had chosen. Their daughter's optimistic and wrongheaded assessment of this young man drove them into frenzy. During her lonely childhood, this young woman's hopeful self was developed in a world of intense fantasy, and the man she selected met her needs by posing as a larger-than-life character. Flamboyant, self-promoting, and grandiose men are the worst possible choice for long-term relationships, however, they fit perfectly into the fantasy world of this young woman's hopeful self.

Blame, responsibility, and revenge are enormous parts of the wounded self, and consequently are of interest to adults who are attempting to break away from their difficult families. In this example, how are we to assess blame? After all, her parents were now trying to help her. During my consultation with them, it became clear that they were completely unaware that their lack of love and support during their daughter's mostly forgotten childhood was responsible for her attraction to an obviously unsuitable man. This example also illustrates the reality that human relationships can be exceedingly complex. The same parents who damaged their child when she was young were now attempting to help her.

We might then say that the young man in this scenario is the villain, but in truth his self-destructive personality is, in all probability, a consequence of his own abandoning, abusive, or neglectful developmental history from his family of origin. Nor was this evolving relational disaster the young woman's fault, as she was operating in the only way she knew how. Her boyfriend was intensely appealing to her because his conscious and unconscious characteristics activated both her hopeful and wounded selves. "Normal" men her age seemed boring and dull, while hostile, grandiose, and overblown men appealed to her.

A fair assessment of this typical scenario forces us to conclude that the young woman's parents are the responsible parties, because they neglected their daughter in the first place. Looking at the lives of young adults who have grown up in unloving families, it is clear that the extent of damage done to their personalities is far greater than the damage from a robbery, a beating, or a mugging—all crimes that would put the offender in jail. However, neither the previously neglectful parents nor the defense-blinded child can identify the source of the problem. These parents had no idea why their daughter fell in love with this unsuitable young man. Their illusion that they provided their daughter with a "good" childhood hid the personality damage they did to her during her developmental years. The young woman is blinded by both the splitting and moral defenses and so she too is unable to locate the source of her problems. They are all faced with a mystery that they do not have the capacity to understand. It is a repeated human tragedy, one that reoccurs almost endlessly, and one that is completely understandable only after recognizing the power of the repressed selves within the human personality. The concept of responsibility usually carries the burden of reparation if one fails to carry out one's responsibilities. This, sadly is not the usual case in human relationships. These parents' earlier failures are somewhat compensated for by the fact that they are now trying to help their daughter. However, there is relatively little that they can do since this, like many human relational tragedies, was the consequence of emotional failures from the past—failures that are no longer apparent, to either the child or the parent. They are attempting to make reparations for errors that they didn't know they were making. Despite the fact that our failed developmental history was our parents' "fault," each of us has the ultimate responsibility for our own life. Those of us who have been victimized by indifference, neglect, or abuse are responsible for the rest of our lives. We must work to understand our histories, to separate as best as we can from those who have hurt us, and to pursue gratifying relationships in the future.

The Collapse of the Hopeful Self

The discussion so far has implied that all undernurtured children end up dependent upon their parents *regardless* of how badly they were treated. This is true up to an extreme point. However, some parents are so indifferent or abusive that even with the use of powerful defense mechanisms the child cannot remain emotionally attached, because there is so little support for a hopeful self to even begin to develop. Tragically, some children who are severely rejected over long periods of time give up all hope of love from their parents. When this happens, the child's entire personality is composed of an enormous revenge-seeking wounded self.

Once the child gives up all emotional attachments to his parents, then his attachments to other members of society suffer as well. Such children experience a continuous internal emptiness and self-hate because they have been discarded by those who should have loved them. The loss of faith in their parents makes them emotionally "unreachable"; often the goodness of others is mocked or attacked. There is a famous story about F. Scott Fitzgerald, the alcoholic author of *The Great Gatsby*, who was walking in Paris with friends when they came upon an old woman who had displayed a tray of handmade pastry and delicate foods at the entrance of her shop. Fitzgerald's friends were admiring the food when he suddenly kicked it over on to the ground. This type of deliberate destruction of another person's best efforts is typical of the rage of the wounded self.

Children and young adults with no emotional attachments to others have nothing to give meaning to their lives, and they look to nonhuman sources for relief and fulfillment: drugs, alcohol, intense impersonal sexuality, or anything else that will blot out the emptiness and inner pain. This tragic result is illustrated in the essay titled "Starving Children," written by Francine Du Plessix–Gray in the *New Yorker*, about her reaction to the movie "Kids":

In the movie "Kids," a band of teen-agers forages for sex, drugs, and booze on New York City streets. The cruelty of these adolescents who taunt gay men and beat up random passersby, the callousness with which they call their girlfriends "bitches" as they paw them into submission, the subhuman grunts and epithets of their speech make the mind reel. I'm still haunted by the shot at the end of the film of their bodies sprawled over one another, like youths brought in for a Roman emperor's debauch, on the floor of a spacious Manhattan apartment. I keep recalling the remains of their daily fodder—liquor bottles and discarded joints, tacos, burritos drenched in pools of salsa—that litter the sight of their orgy. It is that last detail, suggesting their feral, boorishly gulped diet, that somehow comes to mind when one of the film's characters wakes up from his all-night bender in a Manhattan apartment filled with leather furniture and abstract art, looks straight at the camera, and asks, "What happened?"

These children are living demonstrations of the consequences of emotional histories in which all hope for attachment to others has been dashed. They are left with a vast inner emptiness that demands constant distraction and discharge. Emotional starvation and desire for escape from their interior pain is translated into a quest for intense experiences, which are the only types of experiences that are powerful enough to blot out their pain. Their day-to-day reality is dominated by their enormous wounded self, which discharges violence and hate toward those weaker than themselves. Equally importantly, their total disregard for themselves (for they cannot value what their parents discarded), places them and others in repeated physical danger. Let us not forget why these young adults are empty and seething with anger. When they look at themselves they see nothing that was valued by their parents. They have been discarded, and their desire for revenge is a reaction to the treatment they received when they were most vulnerable. These unfortunate children (despite their wealth) are on the path toward self-destruction.

Many readers might find it difficult to feel any pity for these young people. I suspect most would want to punish them, not understanding that they have been enormously punished (if not completely destroyed as human beings) already. Our culture seems incapable of connecting cause and effect when the two events do not occur within easy recall of each other. The parents of these young adults have failed them totally, yet we as a culture refuse to connect cause and effect because we have no stomach for punishing the innocent-appearing parents. The time that has passed between the early years of neglect and the child's outpouring of random hostility in adolescence protects the parents from censure—they can claim their child became involved in "bad company."

Sadly, the young adult is lost in the same cause and effect framework. He or she cannot clearly remember what happened when they were two, three, or four years of age. Worse, the reality of their developmental history has been clouded and denied by the effects of both the splitting and moral defenses. The result of this psychological conspiracy leaves one and only one recourse open for the victim: to unconsciously act out the same destructive pattern with the next generation of child-victims.

THREE

Staying Home

A crisis will occur if any member of the family wishes to leave by getting the "family" out of his system, or dissolving the "family" in himself. Within the family, the "family" may be felt as the whole world. To destroy the "family" may be experienced as worse than murder or more selfish than suicide. Dilemmas abound. If I do not destroy the "family," the "family" will destroy me.

—R. D. Laing

This chapter will examine three young adults who came to therapy because they were unable to leave their families. The developmental principles discussed in the first two chapters are present in all three patients. They were all emotionally undernourished and all remained stuck in their families by the promise of future love and the hidden desire to reform their parents. Similarly, all three used both the splitting and moral defenses, and these defenses, once their salvation, now made their adulthoods all the more difficult.

I have begun with a quote from the late R. D. Laing's essay "The Family and 'The Family,' " because he recognized the seriousness of the emotional damage done to children who were unable to separate from their families. Many unhappy families cling together out of fear rather than out of love or positive attachment. The family members turn to one another in an attempt to protect themselves from the outside world. Often the family impairs the child's developing identity because his or her development is stunted in order to meet the parents' need for protection: "If I do not destroy the 'family,' the 'family' will destroy me." In order to survive as a fully developed adult, the individual from an emotionally impoverished family must give up his attachment to his family ("destroy it" in Laing's terms) in order to save himself. Other members of the family will try to prevent him from leaving because any defection threatens the security of the remaining members. Finally, as I have noted in the first two chapters, the ignored, deprived, or abused child is less likely to escape because his unmet developmental needs keep him attached to his family both for protection from the outside world and to keep his unrealistic hope of love in the future alive.

Three Young Adults Who Needed Help to Escape

This chapter will focus on clinical examples of three of my patients who came for help because they were mired in their families of origin. Generally, those adults with the most deprived emotional histories end up with the very weakest identities, and consequently have to remain closest to their parents in order to function. The case histories in this chapter are ordered from weakest to strongest. The first patient, Julie, an anorexic young woman who continued to live at home and whose daily food intake became the major focus in the family, demonstrates the very weakest personality structure. William, the second example, also still lived at home but functioned marginally (he held a job outside the home) and had a somewhat stronger sense of self, but was still in need of help to free himself. Sandy, the third individual, was in the strongest position of the three as she had enough of an identity to live separately from her parents. However, she could not tolerate the reality behind her illusions, nor could she sever her attachment to her failed parents. Eventually, her defenses, which were originally developed to protect her from the truth about her parents, threatened one relationship after another.

Anorexia: A Failure to Separate

At one time in my practice I was seeing twenty-five people a week, five of whom were suffering from anorexia. This gave me a great deal of experience with this difficult disorder, and the following example is a composite of two of these patients.

At first glance I could see that Julie was seriously anorexic, as the sides of her nose were slightly caved in—a very serious sign of long-term self-starvation. Julie was twenty-six, yet lived at home and was unemployed despite a successful college resume. She described a history in which her needs for self-direction were continually overrun by her mother. When she was young, she had been force-fed, and at other times when she refused to eat, her face had been pushed into her plate. So much damage had been done to her identity by her mother's intrusive attacks on her autonomy (and by her father's refusal to protect her) that she felt too weak to function independently in the world. Anorexia is often described as a disorder of adolescence; however, Julie was twenty-six and her anorexia was a testament to the fact that she remained extremely attached to her destructive family. She had been hospitalized in a treatment program specializing in eating disorders, but soon after her release she went right back home and resumed her self-destructive eating pattern.

Julie had a history of self-punishment when she gained weight, which is common in anorexia and which served as a window into her developmental history. Her body became a representation of her two separate selves (wounded and hopeful) and she related to it in the same way that her parents related to her as a child. When she gained weight, she saw her body from the perspective of her wounded self and disciplined it with a vengeance, often exhausting herself with exercise or purging with laxatives. The intensity of her aggression toward her body informed me of just how punished she once felt when she failed to please her uncompromising mother. Conversely, when she lost weight, she experienced her body from her hopeful self's perspective and felt the possibility of love because of her perversion of the concept of "success" (losing weight when you are severely underweight is a very difficult feat)—despite the fact that her body was in a debilitated state. Her adoration of her looks when she lost weight was a repeated challenge to me, since if I became too critical, she would have left therapy. Julie seemed to jump right out of the pages of Alice Miller's book *For Your Own Good*:

Her parents insist that they have a harmonious marriage, and they are horrified at their daughter's conscious and exaggerated efforts to go without food, especially since they have never had any trouble with this child, who always met their expectations. By the manner in which she is enslaving herself, disciplining and restricting herself, even destroying herself, she is telling us what happened to her in early childhood.   (131)

Miller notes in this powerful passage how the intensity of feelings that were once experienced in childhood are recreated by the anorexic in a single-person drama of her psychological relationship with her mother. Parents of anorexics look like they are deeply involved with the child, but frequently, they are most involved in shaping and training their child's performances, be they academic, athletic, or artistic. They ignore her real needs for closeness, support, and unconditional love. The anorexic child's hopeful self is created out of actual memories of being loved for her brilliant and precocious performances. However, she is fully aware that the love that she receives is fragile and could be destroyed in a second if she fails to live up to her parents' standards. Conversely, her memories of punishment for failure created a large and active wounded self that contains all the anger and pain from the rejections that she experienced. Once again, the splitting defense protected her hopeful self from being contaminated or destroyed by the large number of severe rejections hidden in her wounded self. The heartless way she treated herself when she gained weight served as a mirror into her experience of the rejections that followed her failure to meet her parents' extreme demands.

Julie was almost "welded" to her parents. After our first session, she went home and told her parents everything I had said. This indicated to me that she was fixated at very young age, as she could not maintain any psychological separation from the very people that handicapped her development. Julie also insisted that I get a scale so she could weigh herself in my office. I knew this would place me in the very same position as her parents, struggling week after week over her weight gain or loss. Ironically, her parents, who once dominated Julie, had become her slaves, as they were forced to take care of her long after she should be living on her own. She was once terrified of their disapproval, but now they monitored her food intake and were terrified of her refusal to eat. This pattern of the child learning the parents' tactics and then turning them back against the once dominant adults can be seen again and again in unloving families.

I was determined not to become enmeshed by Julie's weight loss so I bought two high-quality scales and had a mechanically minded friend alter the spring mechanism in one, so it read wildly higher. I proudly displayed my new scale to Julie and as she immediately checked her weight she wailed, "Oh my God, I'm over a hundred pounds!" Julie was around ninety-five pounds at the time. A five-pound gain to an anorexic is psychologically equivalent to a gain of seventy-five pounds to a normal person. "I'm so sorry, Julie," I said, exaggerating my apology. "I bought the scale at a discount house and they said that it might be defective. Bear with me and I will have another one for our next session." Weight was a deadly serious topic to Julie and she was very angry that I could be so casual and incompetent about it. Her weight was her single source of power in the world, and her goal was to use it as tyrannically against me as her mother had used parental power against Julie when she was a child. The next week I had both scales out and told Julie that I wanted to weigh myself as well. She almost grinned—I was obviously playing around with this very serious issue, and I was as determined to have fun as she was to take it seriously. She tried to reassert her power by reciting facts about her altered body chemistry and her precarious hold on life—facts that she knew as well as any medical doctor. This tactic had managed to intimidate the two therapists she had worked with prior to me, but I reasoned that if she managed to dominate our relationship with her weight, then no progress would be possible. "Well, then you use the good scale and I'll use the other one," I said. Julie became uncomfortable with this idea, because weight was her most important weapon in her struggle with the world, and my interest in my own weight threatened to take some attention away from her. *Her* weight was the important issue, not mine. We stood on the scales, side by side, mine reading over a hundred pounds more than hers. She was pleased that my "good" scale matched hers at home, because she weighed herself several dozen times a day. Then I casually slipped my toe on her scale and gave it a little jolt upward. Julie roared, "That's it—I've had it with you! You're making a joke about my very life!" "What life?" I responded. "As far as I can see, you really don't have one." This awful truth spun around the room like a tornado—Julie looked like she was going to faint. "I do so," she protested. "I have a great life—probably better than yours." On and on we went, she claiming that she had a wonderful life except for having to deal with me, her idiotic, bumbling therapist, who was the most incompetent fool she had ever gone to for "help." During her tirade, she was unable to conceal the delight that she took demeaning and condemning me for my incompetence. This helped her indirectly discharge the resentment in her wounded self against her infuriating and incompetent (yet too important to leave) parents. I became the safe symbol for their failure, and Julie excoriated my "technique," my office, my clothing—everything about me. Goodness, did she have fun! We began meeting twice a week and she always started out with a sharp criticism of me—criticisms like the ones she suffered as a child, or those that she heaped on herself if she gained weight: I failed to clear the ice off the walkway endangering the very lives of my patients, there were dust bunnies under the radiators filled with lethal germs, the pictures on the wall were so old they were curling up with shame. On and on these complaints would go until she would segue into her life and struggles with her parents. Gradually, over several years her attacks on me decreased as her new identity took form—an identity that was ultimately strong enough to be able to venture into the world, get a job, and begin an independent life of her own.

William, or Life in the Basement

The majority of adults who fail to separate from their families simply remain at home long after their peers have moved into adult relationships. This is a common scenario, one that occurs in almost every extended family. The following quotation, from Peter Wilson's chapter in the book *Narcissistic Wounds*, illustrates one of the most common signs of impending trouble:

> They have chosen to insulate themselves within an encapsulated inner world, immersed in private preoccupation and phantasy, and occupied in solitary activities. . . . Many drop out of school or work. They give up their studies and literally disappear into their rooms, often staying in bed throughout the day, only occasionally making limited forays out of the house. . . . Their self-imposed isolation of course is not absolute; it occurs in the proximity of others who are inevitably concerned. It functions both to defy and to torment those who are around—and paradoxically to call forth the very interference it seeks to resist.   (55)

The similarity of this description to young women with anorexia nervosa is startling. Both withdraw from normal life within the context of their family, which then focuses more and more (consciously) unwanted attention on the child. Withdrawals during the teenage years indicate that the young adult can not yet face the world outside of the family because they are not yet ready to separate from their destructive but needed parents. Today, many young people who withdraw within the matrix of the family become immersed in science fiction, underground music, or the Internet. I have met others who simply retreated into hours and hours of daydreaming. One patient reported that he invented an entire fantasy town in which he served as the mayor, police chief, and star baseball player.

Those young adults who isolate themselves within the family are tempting their already meddlesome (or in other cases, indifferent) parents to try to vault the now higher wall that they have created. In effect, the young person's wounded self is inviting a fight with the parents. Often, in families where strife is commonplace, the wounded self becomes the major pathway of attachment (motivated by the desire to reform or for revenge) since after years of disappointment the wounded self grows stronger than the hopeful self. When this happens, the young adult usually shifts his efforts toward defeating or defying the needed but hated parent. The troubling aspect of these withdrawals within the family is that the young person's hopeful self's fantasies are often extreme and completely out of touch with reality as compared to the previously described illusions about loving parents. Often, these fantasies are barely based on reality and no longer involve an emotional attachment to others, since these young adults were so deeply disappointed in their parents. In effect, the young adult has given up hope of emotional support from the human community and has substituted grandiose fantasies of unlimited power or fame. This was the case with William, a patient who came for a consultation because he was constantly tired despite sleeping most of the day. He was living in a basement apartment in his parents' home and earning a meager living by stacking shelves in a local supermarket at night. He was at a higher developmental level than Julie because he had a job outside the home; however, he was still developmentally fixated at a preadolescent level and greatly in need of emotional support.

William came in an expensive but old and unkempt suit. He looked like a Beat poet with a long beard and wild and excitable eyes. He had been a high school music teacher but a destabilizing event early in his career forced him to leave that profession, and he took a less stressful job. His supermarket job gave him great freedom from anxiety, since restocking shelves at night afforded few if any interpersonal contacts to upset him. His menial job did not deprive him of income, as his parents supplemented his paycheck every month. He came into therapy both because of his chronic depression and because his dreams of unlimited power were beginning to take on a life of their own. In short, he became concerned that he was going crazy.

William was the only son of European immigrant parents who were once wealthy but were unable to restore their past social and economic status once they came to America. They felt overwhelmed and insecure in this country and disguised their anger and frustration by constantly denigrating everything American while idealizing European culture. William showed enormous promise as a musician at a young age. He attracted considerable attention from his music teachers, who were thrilled to have a student who showed so much obvious talent. Instead of sharing this enthusiasm, his parents were cynical if not outright hostile to his musical achievements, often calling him "the big shot" whenever he reported success in school. His parents unconsciously humiliated their son in order to keep him insecure about his potential. His success threatened to exceed their own achievements in life, which would give them another source of inferiority to face. Had William been encouraged during his development, he would have had enough strength in his identity to separate from his socially inept and insecure parents, begin dating, and perhaps move away, which was another possibility that terrified them. By constantly demeaning him, his parents weakened his identity and prevented him from separating from them. Not unexpectedly, the amount of criticism he faced forced William to develop both the splitting and the moral defense to preserve his attachment to his parents, and the actions of these defenses later proved to be obstacles when he stepped outside his family.

When William applied to colleges, his parents opposed all applications to out-of-state schools, which they deemed too expensive. William complained loudly, but complied, because at some level he too was anxious to separate from the family that had destroyed his confidence in himself. During his college years at a local commuter college, William drew considerable support from his professors and this allowed some positive development of his sense of himself. This newfound strength helped him to challenge (but not separate from) his aggressive and demeaning father. He and his father became involved in a ritualized morning battle. His father would come down to his basement apartment just before leaving for work, seething with irritation because of his chronically oversleeping son. He would demean William as being a lazy "American punk," who fell far short of the family ideal of a cultured and educated young person in the European tradition. In addition to his musical talent, William had a exceedingly quick wit and he would often pester his angry father with entrapping questions. For instance, he would ask whether his father was "first and foremost a Christian, an American, or a man?" His father, who loved contentious debate, would attempt to respond to these loaded questions. Regardless of the answer, William would pick his father's response to shreds. This scene was the reverse of his childhood, where many of William's statements were made fun of by his insecure parents. In effect, this type of questioning became an important part of his attachment to his parents since it helped express the anger in his wounded self. Over time, William became more skilled at this form of hostility than his parents, and he would frustrate and further enrage his already irritated father. On occasion he would so anger his father that the morning confrontation would end with a slap or shove. This reversal is similar to the reversal described in Julie's case, where the child who was enslaved by her parents' every opinion later learns to enslave them by not eating.

After graduation, William's parents bought him a car and suggested that he remain at home rent-free. This sudden switch from hostility to indulgence is common in unloving families, as the parent's tactics shift in order to keep the young adult at home. Many parents are as covertly dependent on their children as their children are on them. William had the option to leave, but the sudden indulgence played into his unmet developmental needs. It seemed as if he was finally getting some of the support he longed for; and second, at some level he realized that his compromised and stunted identity was unable to support him independently in the world. He used the rationalization that he deserved to live rent-free as repayment for all the hostility he had suffered as a child.

His teaching career began with a great deal of promise. During his first year of teaching, William developed several alternative teaching programs for musically gifted students. He showed his outline to several peers who praised its creativity. The praise stimulated his unrealistic hopeful self and he imagined that the Commissioner of Education (who represented a new loving parent) would praise his work. His hopeful self became increasingly grandiose and he began to fantasize that he would revolutionize the teaching of music throughout the country. His hopeful self exaggerated the praise from his colleagues, which substituted for the support that he craved but did not receive from his parents. His imagined success prompted him to make an appointment with a state official in the Department of Education. He assumed it would be a large meeting attended by the Commissioner and his staff. However, when he went to the appointment he was met by a secretary who took his proposal and informed him that they would call him in a few days—a call that never came. His hopeful self collapsed as he was leaving the building and was replaced by his bitter and self-hating wounded self. He heard the words of his father: "the big-shot dreamer," and he seriously thought of suicide as he drove home. By the time he arrived home, he was deeply ashamed of himself and unable to face his colleagues and return to work.

William collapsed into an incapacitating depression, and this reinforced his fundamental belief that he was as defective as his father proclaimed him to be. Not surprisingly, his depression made him docile, and his parents readily offered to take care of him until he was well enough to go back to work. After the one year leave of absence that William was granted expired, he was dismissed by the school. He remained deeply enmeshed within his family of origin, bitter and increasingly angry, yet unable to separate. William displayed the pattern often seen in adults who were undermined as children and consequently are unable to separate from their families: they lead uninspiring and marginal lives and occasionally have momentary flare-ups of unrealistic grandiosity.

William's unhappiness and frustration might lead one to assume that he would welcome help from a mental health professional in his quest to separate from his parents. Nothing could be further from the truth! William brought all of his entrapping questions, his sarcasm, and his absurd grandiosity into his therapy sessions with me. I was confronted with the same type of aggressive questions that so enraged his father. Within the first fifteen minutes of our first session, I felt defensive and frustrated by his verbal onslaught. The enormity of William's wounded self, and his use of it to relate to me, a benign person who is a "designated helper," returns us to the issue of responsibility. His cynical, challenging, and provocative behavior produced the same effect in me as it did in his father. Was William a victim of his history or was he now the perpetrator of his own unsuccessful life? Both positions are true, but as we get older, the responsibility for the conduct of our lives becomes more and more our own burden. By provoking angry responses from others, William was able to recreate a world filled with interpersonal strife and aggression, regardless of the good intentions of the person with whom he was interacting.

After a number of sessions in which I was inundated with hostility and distrust, I became less interested in helping him—a human response that psychologists are supposed to be aware of and overcome. I love to clown around, and suspected that if I could work some fun into our sessions, I would be less likely to give up on William as a patient. I proposed that we keep score of the number of times he really skewered me with his hostile criticisms. I would "rate" his attacks in terms of baseball scoring: singles, doubles, triples or home runs. This strategy took the sting out of his nasty aggression by turning it into a game, and paradoxically, urged William to increase his hostility, so he could achieve a high "score." William replied characteristically, "Sure, any brilliant technique from your grab-bag of flim-flam pseudoscience is fine with me." Within five minutes we were hotly debating the merits of one of his cruel remarks—I had scored it as a double and William felt it was a homer. "Well," I said, "we clearly need to hire a referee." This released another tirade of anger at me, in which he deemed me a "mealy-mouthed weasel that couldn't even score a put-down." I was so taken by his creative contempt that I awarded him a triple on this new attack. This aggressive verbal pattern continued but rather than fighting about me, we were fighting over his creativity. I had moved myself into the role of a judge of his productions rather than as the target. This allowed me to have some fun and to not take his continuous stream of nasty comments to heart. It also allowed us to eventually work cooperatively to begin the process of untangling him from his family. I will return to William in chapter 5.

Sandy: Living Separately—but Alone
The following example of Sandy illustrates the next developmental step upward from William. Sandy is typical of many adults from

developmentally unhelpful families who have been able leave the actual family home, but are unable to prevent the severity of their defenses from disrupting their adult friendships. In effect, Sandy carried such intense and powerful images of her family in her head that she reacted to others as if they were from her family of origin. In psychotherapy, this tendency to react to others as if they are family members is called "transference." Sandy came to see me because of her social isolation, her continuing overwork, and difficulties with the few friendships she had left. She was raised by her divorced mother, a professor of music at a community college. During her childhood, Sandy's mother was frequently physically abusive toward both Sandy and her sister. They were blamed for their mother's disorganized, chaotic, and unsuccessful life. Their mother frequently said that she could have been a world-famous performer had she not been burdened with them. Sandy complained about her intrusive and rejecting mother, yet as an adult her attachment remained intense; she called home daily and she never missed Sunday dinner with her mother, despite describing these family gatherings as "dreadful."

Sandy worked as an editor of screenplays and was financially very successful. However, she was never satisfied with her success and worked at a frenzied pace, constantly looking for a big "break" that would make a name for her in the film industry—just as her mother sought fame in the world of music. Not surprisingly, Sandy was forced by her years of childhood rejection to use the splitting defense in order to remain attached to her mother. This defense became an integral part of her personality that remained into adulthood. The automatic nature of the splitting defense caused her to distort reality by seeing her friends either as extremely good or extremely bad, views which would often change without warning in an instant. This is the great paradox of defense mechanisms: they protect us from crushing anxiety during our childhoods, but then become an integral part of our personality that often damages us in adulthood.

Like many adults who use the splitting defense, Sandy had many relationship problems because the moment she felt frustrated by a friend, her wounded self would jump out of its hiding place in her unconscious and she would "turn" against that person and forget all the good aspects of the relationship. This is just like the child of two who screams "I hate you mommy" just three minutes after cuddling affectionately. Frustration wipes all the positive memories out, and the child is completely caught in the emotions of the moment. These severe shifts of perception and feelings were responsible for many of the relationship breakups that Sandy described. These relationship problems were not limited to male-female romances, as her relationships with other women were filled with strife and she repeatedly got into sudden and unexpected conflicts with a constantly changing cast of friends.

During one session, Sandy described an incident in which she experienced an upwelling of explosive anger toward her current best friend who had "insulted" her sister. Her friend saw a picture of Sandy's sister in the company of a new male companion. The man in the picture was much older than her sister and was dressed like an underworld character. Her friend looked at the picture and exclaimed, "Some catch, I hope he has plenty of money!" Sandy's sudden and extreme anger at this remark took her friend by surprise, because they had often joked about the up-and-down romantic life that Sandy's sister led. Sandy had repeatedly and pointedly made fun of her sister's lifestyle in our sessions as well, describing her as an exploiter of wealthy men who made her "romantic" decisions based on how much money her various dates were willing to spend. Sandy also felt appropriately slighted by the fact that her sister still lived rent-free in the family home, and frequently borrowed large sums of money from their mother without paying it back. This view of her sister came from her wounded self which had a large number of memories of her sister taking advantage of Sandy's good will as well.

I began to investigate what life event prompted Sandy to suddenly switch from her wounded self back to her hopeful self's view of her sister. The answer appeared almost immediately. It was the recent death of her father, a neglectful and completely disinterested parent, who lived in a distant state and had little to do with either of his daughters. The loss of an uninvolved parent should logically have little or no effect on "adult" children; however, because Sandy had never been emotionally supported as a child by either parent, her father's death crushed any remaining hopeful self fantasies she had about him. The attachments to her family that she did have were weak and supported by her unrealistic hopeful self, and the loss of her father increased the need for even stronger fantasies of attachment to her two remaining family members. Her father's passing caused her to strengthen her hopeful self's fantasy that her self-centered mother and exploitative sister constituted a good "family," and simultaneously she repressed her wounded self's perceptions completely.

Thus, the pressure from her father's death provoked her hopeful self to displace her wounded self, and this shift came as a complete surprise to her friend. Her innocent friend had no idea that Sandy was now in a completely different state of mind about her remaining family, and Sandy's harsh reaction astonished and angered her. Sandy's excessive anger was prompted by the fact that her friend's view threatened her now necessary fantasy that she had a close attachment to her sister. Sandy's aggressive response toward her friend caused their relationship to cool dramatically and eventually she lost the relationship.

The suddenness of the anger and its inexplicability often leaves others confused and offended. Sandy felt absolutely justified in her anger toward her friend since she could not remember the opposite view of her sister, which was now repressed in her wounded self. Sandy's use of the splitting defense caused an endless series of "misunderstandings" with friends, which left her without any alternative except to remain attached to her dysfunctional mother and sister. This example illustrates how severe defenses can imperil those few outside relationships that the young adult has, which over time leaves them with fewer and fewer alternative relationships to lean upon. With no network of friendships to support them, and no stable relationship with a partner, many individuals like Sandy continue to lead exceedingly lonely and frustrating lives with only their family to "count" on, a sad fate for many adults who already suffered from destructive developmental histories.

"Repetition Compulsion": Doing "It" Over and Over Again

The greatest irony of a childhood fraught with rejection and frustration is that when the child grows up, he or she tends to recreate similar rejecting and negative situations in his or her intimate adult relationships, assuming the individual even manages to separate from the family of origin. It is the most paradoxical result of a poor developmental history. The recreation of the original family pattern in "new" relationships is a way of remaining attached to the original family in a new location, with new actors in old roles, and this common psychological event is formally called "repetition compulsion." The obvious healthy solution to a painful childhood would be to flee as far as possible from the pain and emptiness of the early years. Often, healthy solutions are out of the reach of adults who were reared in unloving families, because these families were not supportive enough to allow their children to develop new and healthy identities. Rather, these young adults are left with a vast inner emptiness inhabited by the two opposite and unstable wounded and hopeful selves (instead of a complex personality structure), and their relationships with others are marred by both the splitting and moral defenses.

I was originally introduced to the dynamics of selecting the worst possible mate as a consequence of my consulting job to the county public defender, an attorney with the job of representing individuals who could not afford to pay for a lawyer. In most cases, I would administer a battery of psychological tests to the defendant and work with the attorney to aid in the defense. It was in this capacity that I was introduced to a young man who had been arrested for arson—specifically, he had ignited the gas tank of his girlfriend's car as an act of revenge. He explained that his girlfriend had teased him to the point where revenge was his only possible response. I was very surprised to find that every time I called on "Tim" in jail, I saw the young woman whose car he had burned waiting to see him during visiting hours. Later, when he came to my office, she came as well and waited for him in the waiting room. I was puzzled by her attachment to the young man who had deliberately destroyed her car.

Tim described his romance with this young woman, Carrie, as stormy, filled with intrigue, and tremendously exciting. Carrie was volatile and seductive—she would tease him by offering to go out on a date and then deliberately reject him at the last moment. This pattern of promises followed by rejection was unlikely to be popular with many conventional young men, those who are not used to or interested in false promises. However, I was to learn that Tim had been severely rejected by his parents, and he developed a powerful hopeful self that lived on either the illusion of love or its counterpart, the rage within his equally powerful wounded self. Carrie's teasing and enigmatic promises absolutely fascinated Tim, as she appealed to both of his split selves. His hopeful self was activated by her demands that he pass a series of "tests" that proved his love before she was willing to go out with him. These tests provoked long-buried memories of the obstacles he faced when trying to get love from his mother, and they activated his hopeful self, which was sure that love was just around the corner. Conversely, his wounded self was used to severe rejection, and when rebuffed, Tim worked strenuously to overcome and reform Carrie's resistance to dating him, just as all children initially try to get their parents to pay attention to them. Not surprisingly, Tim had been indifferent toward a past girlfriend who had freely given him affection because it did not feel genuine to him.

The more unreasonable the demands that Carrie placed on Tim as a prerequisite to her surrendering her (assumed) love, the more he became emotionally involved. Carrie's rejections were humiliating and quite severe, and his wounded self, with its enormous desire to reform the other, was engaged and working at fever pitch. He had a preexisting program of strategies designed to change his girlfriend's mind when she rejected him. His hopeful self also was completely engaged by Carrie's promises, which he assumed signaled that she had a storehouse of love waiting to be tapped, although this was on the basis of no evidence whatsoever. The more bizarre, unreasonable, and sadistic Carrie's behavior became, the more Tim was attracted to her. At this point, early in my career, I realized I was in new territory, and went to my supervisor for a lesson on the dynamics of the human unconscious.

Carrie stepped over the line and became so rejecting that Tim's wounded self gave up on all efforts to reform her, and in a torrent of frustration he switched to a revenge scenario. Carrie overstepped Tim's tolerance when she deliberately invited another interested young man to her home after she had also agreed to see Tim, knowing that this would make him jealous. Tim went into a rage, punctured her car's gas tank with a screwdriver, and ignited the gasoline, burning himself in the process. Ordinary women would be horrified by the hostility of this behavior but Carrie saw his antisocial act as a tribute to her value and to her power.

After he was jailed, Carrie behaved like a devoted family member. She saw Tim as being more powerful and desirable than ever before. Her adoring response provoked Tim to switch back to his hopeful self, and the intricate selection process that underlies repetition compulsion was well on its way. Their mutual hopeful selves were cut off from the memories of her sadism and his violent revenge. Both Tim and Carrie had two isolated and opposite selves that engaged each other in an elaborate dance that not only focused all their energies on each other, but also excluded normal individuals from being interested in either one of them. This emotional drama engaged all of the preexisting mechanisms of both of their personalities. In simplest terms, Tim's childhood prepared him for this type of relationship, as he could not feel comfortable with a normal partner who would be unable to engage these large unconscious parts of his personality. He found Carrie's rejections as challenging as were his parents' rebuffs. His wounded self churned inside him, filled with desires of revenge or reform, while his hopeful self was filled with the expectation of unlimited love. Tim believed that Carrie, who was in reality a bizarre and dysfunctional woman, was a prize catch, and he pursued her with the same zeal that he pursued his original parents. This is the same dynamic that is responsible for the endless attachment between the battered woman and her abuser that I have detailed in my book *The Illusion of Love: Why the Battered Woman Returns to Her Abuser.*

FOUR

Preparing for Change

The truth which makes men free is for the most part the truth which men prefer not to hear.

—*Herbert Agar*

The first three chapters detailed the development of the human defenses that keep us bound to our families and interfere with our adulthood functioning. Now our emphasis will shift to the first step on the road to recovery: defeating and overcoming those defenses. Up to now, the major focus has been on the "badness" of the parents. However, change has to come from within the self, and therefore the focus will be on activities, behaviors, and attitudes that we must work to change if we are to succeed in separating ourselves from our families of origin.

Controlling the Anger in Our Wounded Selves

The wounded self's eagerness to assign blame can maintain the angry attachment between this wounded part of our personality and our failed parents, either through the desire to reform them or to seek revenge. Getting beyond this point is essential, because after we succeed in renouncing blame, the role played by our wounded self is reduced, as is our fascination with the "badness" of others. This frees us to develop relationships with others who truly appreciate our qualities. Sadly, many developmentally deprived adults are so intent on assigning blame that they end up behaving like psychological policemen, intent on pursuing those that have failed to live up to their childlike ideals. As I have noted in the "responsibility" section of chapter 2, it is true that our parents were responsible for the failures we experienced in childhood. However, unlike traffic court, where there are assigned fines for a variety of irresponsible behaviors, parents often "violate" the rules of acceptable parenting with no censure from society. They fail as parents because of their own childhoods, which may have filled their personalities with unconscious motives that they blindly reenact. Secondly, their "crimes" against the healthy development of their children were committed when they were somewhat different people, in different situations. And perhaps the most difficult point of all to accept, even when we have reached adulthood, is that our parents were limited, either by their intelligence, their primitive emotions, their poverty of either money or love, or by other circumstances beyond their control. My patients find this concept hardest to grasp because it shatters the illusion in the hopeful self that their parents' love was somehow available to them, if only they through some behavior of their own could access it. Often, it simply was not available and no amount of arguing, cajoling, teaching, or begging would have changed their impaired parents.

One of the dangers of our wounded self is that it was created during our early development, and it contains both memories of events and the emotional attitudes we had in that stage. The memories are invaluable—however, bringing the attitudes of a young child into an adult life can be dangerous. That is, as children, we all carried an inflated view of our parents' importance. In adulthood it is crucial to know who is truly important and who is not. The mature adult will accept the reality that his or her random birth into an unloving family was simply a stroke of bad luck and move on, without seeking revenge or compensation. The psychologist Sheldon Kopp recognized that many of his adult patients could not give up their anger at being "cheated" out of a good childhood. In the following quote from *An End to Innocence*, he comments on his patients' wounded selves, which are invariably filled with the desire for revenge:

> Imagining themselves to be the heroes or heroines of as yet un-completed fairy tales, such people simply cannot (will not) believe that the villains who have disappointed them will go unpunished, or that they themselves will remain blameless yet uncompensated victims. Surely there must be someone who will avenge them, and take good care of them, someone who will right the family wrongs and reward the good children. (38)

This strong, but absolutely true statement reflects what I have en-countered with many of my patients. Many develop a sense of in-flated self-importance in reaction to overwhelming feelings of infe-riority and abandonment. Many of us cannot accept our bad luck as simply a random event in a random universe, but instead expe-rience our emotional pain as if it is the single most important issue in our life. In reality, this exaggeration of our importance, along with our wounded self's hope to reform or to get revenge, are fan-tasies that protect us from the even more frightening possibility that there is no justice when it comes to our families. In reality, there is no one to come in and clean up the family mess, and the longer we remain home, waiting for salvation or enmeshed in the daily dramas, the less able we will be to begin life anew. Every day spent trapped in a unloving family erodes our confidence in our-selves. After many years of waiting for the miracle that never hap-pens, we may become too convinced of our own weakness to even try to escape.

Often, patients who view the world through the eyes of their wounded selves assume that all potential sources of support have secret vulnerabilities (just like their parents had) that will disap-point them and ultimately destroy any relationship that develops. This eagerness to blame others keeps our attention fixed on the outside world and away from our role in choosing to remain in frustrating relationships with others, either with our parents or in new, equally difficult adult friendships. The concept of repetition compulsion, discussed in chapter 3, described how we unconscious-ly choreograph one disappointing adult relationship after another. Thus blaming others is a futile proposition, since the real solution is for us to pull away from those we complain about and involve our-selves in more satisfying relationships with healthier "others."

In many of my older patients, the relationship between the hope-ful self and the wounded self changes, with the wounded self view of the world becoming dominant. This is understandable, given the large number of failed interpersonal relationships that their uncon-scious repetition compulsion led them into during their adulthood. As their wounded selves became more and more dominant, many developed an increasingly large "chip on the shoulder" about the possibility of a successful relationship in the future. The following patient history of Charlie illustrates this common emotional trap.

Charlie came for his first appointment wanting to know what I thought of his difficulties with women. He was a member of a re-covery group and dated women exclusively from this subculture, which brought him into contact with women who had very diffi-cult developmental histories. He had brought a notebook that con-tained a list he had made of the women he had dated, and he began with the first woman on his list. He described, in minute detail, her every shortcoming, from her childlike tantrums to her frequent and humiliating struggles with depression. When he was finished, I began to make a comment, but he waved his hand imperiously in-dicating he had more material and could not be interrupted. I was somewhat put off by his gesture, but remained silent and heard the failings of the next person on his list, a well-known real estate salesperson. He eagerly reported that she was secretly still drinking and took "business trips" to Las Vegas where she gambled until she was deeply in debt. Charlie presented his wounded self's condem-nations with an edge of moral outrage that prevented me from try-ing to soften his position. I had much to say by the time he finished exposing the deceptive realtor, but I was not given the chance. Charlie immediately moved on to his third example of a failed re-lationship, which was slightly different in that it was a professional one: a physician who had failed to note his symptoms of drug abuse. This type of statement is often considered to be a disguised criticism of the therapist and is called a "derivative." However, it was our first session and we were not ready to explore this avenue. When Charlie finished his expose, I assumed that I would finally be able to get a word in, but he seamlessly shifted to a remarkably inaccurate self-assessment in which he described himself to be a philosopher and an astute student of the human condition.

I am usually optimistic when I meet a patient for the first time, but in this case I was concerned that Charlie was going to be a very difficult patient. This pattern continued for the next two sessions. Charlie continued to dominate our conversations, expounding at length on his girlfriends' shortcomings, rarely listening to me, when indeed he did give me an opportunity to speak. During our fourth session, I finally began to get some specific details of Charlie's childhood, which he defensively described as "perfect," but to my ear was filled with parental failures. Within a day of that session, he had left a message on my answering machine canceling therapy because I struck him as a "fly-by-night psychologist." It was obvious to me that the moment we shifted our focus to his developmental history and were no longer looking at the failings of the women in his current or past romantic relationships, he sensed danger. He could not tolerate the possibility of tarnishing his hopeful self's illusory view of his parents. Charlie's fragile identity required the support of "good parents" and in order to keep them pure, he directed all of the anger in his wounded self toward his current relationships. The hostility in his wounded self was always directed at expendable women, thus insuring that it never damaged the fantasies that he had about his family of origin. All of his contempt was directed at safe (non-family) targets.

This extreme use of the splitting defense allowed Charlie's wounded self to freely discharge his childhood disappointment at current or past lovers or professionals who failed him, while his parents remained frozen in the illusory gaze of his hopeful self. Charlie was so defensive at this time in his life that he felt he was not an appropriate candidate for psychotherapy, and his fear of the truth caused him to terminate. This does not mean that all hope is lost. Over time, he may return to another therapist and venture another look at his history and parents. The lesson for all of us provided by Charlie is to be wary of an overly powerful and self-righteous wounded self, particularly when it is solely focused on condemning others. As noted previously, the wounded self can be a valuable tool when it is properly understood, because it contains important memories that are crucial in the unraveling of our personal histories. However, when the wounded self dominates us and we ignore the effect of our own role in creating our current relationships, we face the possibility that our entire personality can become embittered and vengeful. Carefully and accurately assessing our wounded self can allow us to make use of its valuable material without getting carried away by its anger and its desire for revenge.

I am not pretending for a moment that the world at large does not cause us problems. There are the absolute realities of economic problems, the possibility of random physical injuries, illnesses, and all sorts of other catastrophes that can afflict us. However, relationship problems, particularly repeated patterns of struggles with others or long lists of disappointments in others, do not come out of "nowhere." They are the product of careful unconscious engineering, as dramatically illustrated by Tim and Carrie from the previous chapter, who found each other through an act of arson.

There exists another defense that must be conquered before we can escape from our family: the illusions we have about ourselves. Sadly, it is as hard to give up our illusions about ourselves as it is to give up on the illusions we create about the goodness of our parents. Self-centeredness is one of the more destructive consequences of a neglectful childhood; a childhood that required the use of extreme defenses to survive from day to day. Self-centeredness is a consequence of the continued deprivation of our needs, to the point that our internal deprivation becomes the focus of our life. Many children are so focused on getting their reasonable needs met that their identity develops around the emotional traumas that they suffered, like a tree that grows around a wire fence. The resulting personality often is bereft of healthy optimism, of trust in others, or even "normal" friendliness. The resulting damage to our personalities is often very unappealing to others. Equally importantly, an honest assessment of ourselves becomes more difficult because the type of negative information we have to hear and accept about ourselves seems to come from people we dislike and demean.

Thus young adults from deprived or neglectful histories are often exceedingly one-sided and selfish. The self-centeredness is part of a ongoing attempt to meet unmet childhood needs, while the aggression toward others protects the individual from the humiliations that he or she expects at every turn. One of the most common self-deceptions that I see in my practice is the single male who is seething with self-righteous hostility, but sees himself as a "nice guy." These young men are completely unaware of their powerful wounded self, which is the most potent and obvious part of their personality. For instance, Gary, a student of mine, came for therapy after finally graduating from college. He had taken six years to finish his undergraduate degree because his wounded self targeted the authorities at the university as a symbolic family that he was determined to reform in ways that would meet his exacting needs. His career as a reformer began when he was called into the dean's office to alter his course schedule. Gary was a biology major but he insisted on taking four different history courses during one semester, ignoring the requirements for his major. During the conference with the dean, Gary argued against the university policy that required students to take a specified number of courses every semester in their major. He found a local attorney who had a separate reason for wanting to sue the university and who agreed to work with Gary for a nominal fee. Much of Gary's time was spent challenging the policies and procedures that had been established by the university administration, and he was so enthralled by his mission that he took time off from his schoolwork in order to work with this attorney. He and his attorney instigated a series of lawsuits challenging the various policies regarding curriculum, student life, and even tuition. These lawsuits gave Gary local notoriety and for a short time he became a student celebrity. He was so excited about his sudden importance that his ambitions became more grandiose and distorted, and he began to look at local politics as a way of maintaining his new-found status. He entered therapy a year after graduation because his life had suddenly collapsed when his wounded self no longer had the university as a target for its hostility and his political career failed to get off the ground. He began one session by saying that "all of the meaning of life seemed to drain away the moment I left school." His struggle with the school authorities was an almost exact recreation of his childhood struggle with his parents—however, this time his struggle afforded him temporary status and importance that was denied him in childhood.

Gary initially presented himself in therapy as a relaxed "nice guy" who had chosen me because he had enjoyed the lectures in my undergraduate abnormal psychology class. He seemed interested in exploring his history and relationship dynamics, and he was so pleased at the results of our first session that he asked for another appointment for the very next day. I explained that this was not possible because other patients had regular appointments. He became very angry and accused me of being a rigid elitist who was out to exploit him for his money. This was the very first salvo of what was to become an ongoing attack on me, originating in his wounded self, which jumped from his unconscious into his awareness the moment I was unwilling to meet his needs. Gary's fast shifts from admiration to hostility were classic signs of the splitting defense. He shifted from idealization (that is, seeing me through the eyes of his hopeful self) to denigration the moment I frustrated his needs. Frustration of his voracious needs was incompatible with idealization and it unconsciously reminded him of his unending childhood deprivation at the hands of his parents. Frustration provoked his wounded self to emerge from his unconscious and displace his hopeful self. As his hopeful self receded, the view of me as potentially helpful and good was swept away. His view of me changed from a parental substitute who promised support and love to one who offered nothing but frustration and neglect.

When Gary was dominated by his wounded self, he became a very unappealing human being. His wounded self was awash in childhood feelings of deprivation and these prevented him from seeing that he had become an arrogant, infantile adult who always wanted to be first, regardless of the needs of others. Not surprisingly, his behavior seemed to be very similar to his description of his father. Often, the extreme emotions contained in the wounded self destroy our social skills and our sensitivity to others, because the emotions we feel seem so genuine and compelling. The vividness and power of these feelings gives us the illusion that we have license to act harshly, when in reality, the intensity comes from the ancient frustrations that have been stored up for years. In order to escape from our defenses, we must develop enough trust in others to allow their views of our behavior to penetrate our awareness. In the example of Gary, my view of his personality as being self-centered and selfish was completely alien to his view of himself as a self-sacrificing hero who was trying to protect his fellow students from a brutal and callous university administration. The strength of his emotions convinced him that he was a visionary and that the world was deaf and dumb to his efforts on behalf of others. I will finish the story of my work with Gary in chapter 5.

A second caution we should heed is for us to be wary of the emotional strength of the memories buried in the wounded self. These emotions are reflections of our *original* reactions to painful family events. These ancient emotional reactions remain unchanged despite the time that has passed since the traumatic events took place, and consequently, the emotions can be very strong when they emerge. Just as we must recognize that our hopeful selves are unreliably optimistic, we must also accept the fact that our wounded selves are unrealistically angry and vengeful. The memories of neglect and abuse recorded in our wounded selves actually occurred, but the accompanying emotions are only appropriate for the time and place during our development when they were first experienced. We were so vulnerable and helpless when we were subjected to either neglect or abuse that we felt that our life was being threatened, and our emotional reactions match this extreme level of perceived danger. These ancient emotions tell us, for instance, how a child of six feels about being forgotten in a store. If that child could have retaliated with the strength of an adult, he or she might have severely beaten their abandoning parent.

The anger within the wounded self is the likely source of the recent rash of school murders committed by teens and preteens. Children with enraged wounded selves do not recognize that the strength of their feelings come from an earlier time. Rejection by schoolmates is not life-threatening, but to a two- or three-year-old, parental rejection *feels* that way. The young person simply substitutes current rejection at school for past rejections and unleashes the rage from an earlier time. The recent increase in this kind of lashing-out behavior may be due to the easy access to weapons and the universal exposure to what I call "instructional videos." The action movie genre depicts invincible superheroes who seek revenge (usually with deadly automatic weapons) against those who have wronged them. The protagonist is always "in the right" and never suffers any negative consequences for his murderous rampage. Many preteen children are burdened by large wounded selves and loaded with early rage from emotional abandonment, and these feelings sometimes are translated into deadly action. The wounded self takes actions that seem incomprehensible to the outside observer. The lesson, once again, is that the truths stored in our wounded selves are mixed with powerful feelings of rage that no longer apply to our adult situations.

Accepting the Painful Truths in Our Dreams

Not all patients are alike. Charlie indulged in the desire for revenge against all who offended him, all the while still protecting the fantasy that he had "good" parents. Gary was different than Charlie, in that he had no illusions about his family. However, he indulged the anger in his wounded self and created the illusion of himself as a justice-seeker. Other patients are quite different still. Many are fearful of any contact with their wounded selves. Often, these individuals are still closely connected with their families and cannot tolerate to see negative aspects of their parents.

I have detailed the dangers of acting on the worst aspects of our wounded selves, and now it is time to highlight the positive, therapeutic help that this part of our personality can provide us. The great strength of our dreams is the ability of our unconscious to tell us the truth by jumping over our normal waking defenses. Understanding our dreams can be one of the most powerful ways to get beyond our carefully constructed defenses.

When I work with a patient like Charlie who describes a whole series of failed adult relationships, I understand this material as being equivalent to an X-ray of their early failed relationships with their parents. The hidden truth the patient and I must uncover is the nature of the failings of his parents that he is unable to remember or acknowledge, so that ultimately, he can accept those failings. I approach this mystery through a careful and detailed examination of the patient's childhood. If a patient complains of an endless series of failed love relationships, I begin by asking about his family of origin. This question often seems impertinent to the patient because his defenses keep the connection between his childhood relationships and his adulthood relational problems in completely separate categories. Very rarely will a patient reveal a pain-filled developmental history. Does this imply that I "make up" a story filled with deprivation and unrecognized hurts and then convince my patients that they were actually wounded in order to explain the inability to separate from their families? On the contrary. It is the patient who gradually reveals bits and pieces of his history that, up to now he dares not see. The powerful presence of the therapist who acts like a "substitute" parent by offering support can sometimes allow the patient to face hidden realities that were too difficult to face alone.

Luckily, even the most defensive patients have an ace in the hole: their ability to dream. Dreams are one of our greatest allies in the search for the truth about our developmental histories, because our wounded selves often speak to us directly, allowing us to "see" painful realities that we consciously deny. The following two dreams came from patients whose wounded selves knew the truth about their families but could not admit it, because they could not yet afford to live without their hopeful selves' illusions. That is, a clear assessment of the material in the wounded self as expressed in dreams, particularly when validated by a dispassionate observer like the psychologist, would destroy the illusions in the hopeful self.

Angie came from a large working-class family of six children. Her father ran a rural hardware and farm supply store and used his children as employees long before they were able to master the tasks that they were expected to do. Angie was particularly good with numbers and she was given the job of bookkeeper when she was only eleven. She was also required to wait on customers and drive a large flatbed truck to pick up grain, hay, and feed at mills in the area, years before she had a driver's license. She was terrified when she had to take on an adult jobs without any help, but she had no one to validate those feelings and perceptions. Driving the farm truck was particularly frightening because she was too short for her feet to touch the pedals. Every time she had to press the brake, she was forced to slide down the seat and therefore could not see out of the windshield. Her father did not pick on Angie specifically; all the children in the family were exploited in similar ways. Angie's mother, however, did single her out as the "bad child" and physically abused her, often out of her own frustration. As a consequence, Angie spent much of her childhood hiding from her mother. She had no one to complain to, and in fact she and her siblings were told that they were enjoying wonderful childhoods. The complete lack of validation of her perceptions forced her accurate memories of callous exploitation to remain isolated in her wounded self. As a young adult, she found herself attracted to enormously difficult jobs in which there were extremely high standards of performance and in which she was given no help or direction, an exact unconscious re-creation of her childhood. She worked at a furious pace and was emotionally unavailable to others because of her frenetic work schedule. The one anomaly in her closed emotional life was her dog, upon whom she poured out all her love. One of her concerns was the extraordinarily intense feelings she had for her dog—feelings that were more intense than those for her husband or any other human in her environment. On the session before Thanksgiving, she came in completely shocked by a dream she had just the night before. Her parents, like many that I have previously described, demanded homage from their adult children, even though they had failed to nurture them during their critical developmental years. Every year, the children would each prepare part of the Thanksgiving meal, and then gather at their parents' home to celebrate. Angie's dream was that she was required to kill, butcher, and cook her dog, and present him as her contribution to the family Thanksgiving dinner. She was appalled and dumbfounded that her unconscious could think up such a horrible fate for the single living thing in the world that she loved the most.

Angie had been a resistant patient prior to this session. She made excuses for her continuing attachment to parents who never ceased exploit her. I made a simple interpretation: her dream was telling us both that her wounded self knew that she had been treated badly in childhood. Her wonderful, loving, and loyal dog represented herself as a child, and her dream was saying that she recognized that her innocent trust and love for her parents had been "sacrificed" to their self-centered needs. In adulthood, her suspicion of others (including her husband) caused her to focus all her love on her dog—the only living creature to whom she dared to expose the full force of her affectionate, positive feelings. This example shows us that Angie's repressed wounded self was able to express itself in ways that her consciousness (which was dominated by her hopeful self) was not able to prevent.

Our need for our parents, when combined with our terror at facing all of the hurt and anger stored in our wounded selves, forces many of us to keep accurate perceptions of our childhood plight limited to dreams. In Angie's case, it was the fear of feeling intensely abandoned by her family that would follow if she accepted the reality of the rage and grief in her wounded self. In the following example of Sarah, it was her continuing financial and emotional dependency on her mother that forced her to erect reality-distorting defenses that prevented her from consciously acknowledging her pain. However, her wounded self came to her aid in therapy, and produced a dream that was a beautifully recorded and truthful snapshot of her relationship with her mother.

Sarah was a twenty-five-year-old graduate student who was the daughter of a wealthy urban real estate developer and a socialite mother. Sarah had been alternately controlled and ignored by a mother who spent most of her time and effort on the cocktail circuit, where she was admired for her physical beauty. Sarah was exceedingly bright, but the neglect that she experienced did not allow a clear sense of identity to develop. Her mother used her as a prop when her social life required a daughter, but otherwise she ignored Sarah. When she was a teenager, she tried to escape through indiscriminate drug use and once, through a failed suicide attempt. When she married, her mother took complete control of the wedding plans and made all of the decisions. In therapy with me, Sarah reported a dream about the rehearsal dinner: All of her mother's friends were present, but none of her own. Her mother had been drinking and was holding forth at the end of the table while Sarah sat silently on display as the good daughter. Her mother began playing a campfire game, in which a utensil was placed on the table and a knife was crossed over it and struck on the end. This launched the knife into the air and it arced toward Sarah and pierced her skull. During the dream she was aware that this was a typical scene: her mother was showing off and having fun, while she remained quietly on display as the good daughter, and was injured as a result.

These two dreams are straight out of the wounded self. Neither of these young women were given enough security to separate from their families and so could not give up the illusions nursed in their hopeful selves. Their wounded selves were never allowed to express their experiences of hurt, anger, and pain to the adults in their worlds, and the truth about their childhood had to be isolated and ignored. Luckily, both were able to accept these hidden realities with support and encouragement. For a person not in therapy, the valuable truths contained in the wounded self are not seen as credible, as they frequently emerge during moments of temper, in frightening dreams, or through vague feelings of dread. As a consequence, many of us distrust, dislike, and avoid this part of ourselves because it disrupts our attachment to our needed families. Katherine Ann Porter's essay, quoted in chapter 1, noted that many of us see the existence of our wounded selves as a "black treacherousness," but in fact it can be a psychological gold mine if we understand it properly and allow it to speak.

Overcoming Self-Blame from the Moral Defense

As I have noted, not all patients are alike. Those patients who over-use their abused selves and condemn others are less likely to use the moral defense, which blames them while saving the "goodness" of others. Conversely, those individuals who are less aware of their wounded selves often rely on the moral defense to keep them attached to their families and accept all the blame for the failure of relationships. This defense helped them to remain unaware of the extent of the damage being done by their rejecting family while growing up and continues to undermine many patients in their adulthood.

The two groups of patients vary because one group relied on the moral defense during their childhood, while the other used the splitting defense. In adulthood, the self-blame group will admit to all sorts of real and imagined failings: perhaps they aren't loving enough, or they are too selfish, or not intellectually sparkling enough to attract the right kind of partner. Many patients who use this defense present themselves as if they are a "bad seed"; they see themselves as the faulty offspring of healthy parents, thus sacrificing their sense of "goodness" to preserve the fantasy that they had loving and supportive parents. The use of the moral defense is particularly destructive later in life because it poisons our self-esteem, as it constantly blames us for all interpersonal failures while simultaneously exonerating the guilty parties. It's the psychological equivalent of a jailer who frees all the criminals and jails the innocent.

An example of a person struggling to overcome his own use of the moral defense can be seen in the writings of psychologist Sheldon Kopp, whom I quoted earlier in this chapter. The following quotes come from his book, *An End to Innocence*:

Bemuddled by years of immersion in an atmosphere of family hypocrisy, I had emerged from adolescence believing that I was an awful, inadequate human being who went around making other people unhappy. It was the only way I could account for being condemned by people as honest and good as my parents. I entered therapy to be cured of whatever failings had warranted their condemnation.   (86)

Kopp displays the typical attitude of the patient who, at the beginning of the therapeutic process, overuses the self-blame defense to protect his attachment to his parents. At this early stage of his development, he was unable to see that his highly idealized parents were not "honest and good" but were in fact rejecting and abusive. Healthy and loving parents would have never condemned him the way his dysfunctional parents did—a truth hidden from him by the moral defense. Kopp describes his childhood as a mixture of rejection of his real needs interspersed with indulgences that did not help him mature. He was given what his parents wanted to give him but not what he needed for his development. Worse, his very being was defined as defective by his mother when she claimed that he was not a member of the family:

> Over and over she told me that there *must* have been a mix up at the hospital. Surely some other lucky mother must have taken home the good baby with which she should have been blessed. Now she was stuck with the wrong child. "I love you, but I don't like you," she would tell me. Even though I was an undesirable changeling, she would try to raise her little frog as though he were a prince. (70)

Kopp's life story illustrates once again that emotional abuse can undermine the developing child's identity as surely as physical abuse. Psychological terms are completely unnecessary in the analysis of this passage. Kopp's mother was insulting, humiliating, and demeaning. He was blamed for something in which he had no role. Kopp boldly describes the results of this type of covertly hateful parenting on the development of his personality. He spent his youth on the edges of society in the company of misfits, since his identity was too damaged to allow him to live a normal life. Over a number of years, he struggled to rid himself of his shame and sense of defectiveness and his efforts resulted in a stunning and brutally honest conclusion about his childhood:

> Until I was twenty I had believed that my family had shamed and punished me because I was a bad child who had made everyone

unhappy. With the help of my first therapist I gradually came to understand instead that the only reason I had been mistreated was because my mother hated me, and because my father did not care enough to intervene. (90)

Every time I read this quotation I am struck by the power of Kopp's clear statement that his mother hated him. It is not the type of indictment that is often spoken in our culture. More importantly, it is not an easy reality to accept, even in someone whom we have never met. It is shocking both because of the pain that it contains for the person who is able to admit this reality, and for the pain in our own wounded selves that is called up by his confession.

It is difficult to imagine an individual coming to this conclusion without therapy. Kopp's painful but accurate assessment of his history left him dangling over the edge of a psychological cliff, because implicit in his discovery was the reality that his attachment to his family was a self-created illusion. He needed the fantasy of good parents more than his parents needed him as a child. Kopp's revealing psychological journey illustrates that it takes enormous strength of character, plus strong attachments to a supportive network of intimates and friends, for anyone to reach this frightening (but enormously freeing) conclusion about their family. The alternative is worse—for as long as self-blame from the moral defense remains in power, we will remain attached to others who abuse or demean us.

Holding a Clear Vision of Our Parents, Despite Guilt

In my discussion of George, the youthful thief, I noted that the conflict between loving a parent and feeling anger toward them constituted an almost unsolvable conflict. This conflict does not disappear over time. Many adults from unloving families were forced into the role of "parent" by their actual parents, who were incompetent, needy, and unable to face many of life's tasks. The child often ends up feeling that his or her parents' very life depends on their support. Many of my adult patients report that they remain home because they cannot tolerate the guilt that would engulf them if they separated from their hopeless and helpless parents. The following quote from a patient of Joan Raphael-Leff, from her chapter in the book *Narcissistic Wounds*, illustrates a point I made in the first chapter, which is that the inability to hold on to a single clear view of our parents will prevent us from taking any action to save ourselves:

> Visiting my parents I realized how much of the time I was seething with unexpressed rage. My mother arouses such mad, intense feelings in me—she watches me all the time and is so anxious and over involved with everything I do—even when I breathe I feel she'll pounce and tell me I'm doing it wrong. She makes me feel I don't know who I am or what's real or what belongs to whom. I was meant to be someone else. It always seemed the person I am has no right to exist. I'm a husk, my liveliness scooped out by her like a mealworm. It makes me want to murder her—then I feel so monstrous for killing her off. As a tiny child I felt handcuffed to her—chained by her overprotectiveness and my guilt. She didn't talk to me but used to sigh a lot and I was convinced that her absolute anguish must be my fault. Only when I was older did I realize she was depressed, mourning my sister I never knew existed. I was the ghost and my sister was real to her. I want to find myself but seeing how vulnerable and fragile she is I still seem compelled to do everything I possibly can to be who she wants and make up for her tragic life—and when I leave, I feel I'm taking away from her everything she needs for her survival.   (84)

This patient is caught in the conflict between love and anger, as a result of her childhood role of rescuer. Her hopeful self became obsessed with its rescue mission, while her wounded self became filled with anger because it recognized she was being stunted by a mother who too deeply depressed (and therefore, self-absorbed) to meet her legitimate developmental needs. In reality, her mother related to her as if she were a ghost, because she was unable to mourn a lost child, the sister of the speaker, who died before she was born.

This patient's complex and conflicted childhood is reflected by the series of mutually incompatible views of her mother, based on the splitting defense. This defense, combined with the emotional deprivation she suffered as a child, precluded the development of a strong identity. Her lack of courage in her own perceptions left her unable to hold on to a single clear view of her childhood. The resulting confusion does not leave her with enough conviction to take any single path of action. A careful look at the quotation reveals that she speaks from both her wounded and hopeful selves as well as from a realistic adult perspective. Her wounded self is dominant when she says that she is so angry that she could murder her mother because of the intrusive, autonomy-destroying control and deprivation that she suffered. Soon after the murder statement, her adult sense of reality steps in and condemns herself for thinking of killing a pathetic and innocent woman who needs help. Then she switches to her hopeful self in her statement of her desire to rescue that same mother, who remains important to her because her hopeful self still believes that her mother contains the potential for future love. The moment her hopeful self wins this tug-of-war and she spins the fantasy that she can rescue her mother, it is immediately contradicted by her adult view that recognizes that she will have to sacrifice her own individuality in the process. What is certain here is that this continued conflict between the opposite feelings from her hopeful and wounded selves will allow confusion to prevail and prevent any assertive, positive action, while time continues to slip by.

If this patient were able to discard her two hidden selves she would be able to see that there is precious little left to her "relationship" with her mother. *Our hopeful selves are masters of illusion, and they convince us that love exists in people who haven't expressed a single bit of love toward us during their entire lives.* The moral defense tells us that it is our fault that we were neglected, and it combines with the hopeful self, and convincing us that if we are good, loving, and persistent enough in our rescue efforts, our self-centered parents will finally offer us their hidden storehouse of love. Conversely, our wounded self assures us that if we fight hard enough against our rejecting parents (or adult lovers) we can either reform them or at least enjoy a measure of revenge by destroying their evilness. In essence, our defenses create a endless cascade of illusions: the illusion that we live in a rational world, the illusion that we have loving parents, and finally the illusion that if we fight against those family members who have wronged us, justice will prevail.

Given the proper support, this patient might be able to hold on to the reality of the simple observation that her mother was so grief-stricken about the loss of her older sister that she was unable to care for her, and then she could begin the process of freeing herself from this destructive attachment to a failed parent. As things stand however, the guilt she displays at the end of the quotation reduces the possibility of change. When her mother dies, she will find herself in the frightening world of adults with no experience on how to navigate.

I have noted that novelists know just as much about human psychology as members of my profession, and once again I turn to a novelist to illustrate the tragic consequence of remaining loyal to a failed parent. This quotation is from *The Cunning Man*, a novel by Robertson Davies. The speaker is a mature physician describing a older woman patient who has endless psychosomatic complaints:

> Miss Fothergill was more of a nuisance than most of my patients, not because of any complexity in her case but because her resistance was uncommonly strong; she fought me every inch of the way at every consultation, because she was convinced she knew how the world wagged. . . . At the age of fifty-three she was alone, as her mother had died a few months before she came to see me. . . . Old Burton would have described her illness as Maids', Nuns', and Widows' Melancholy, but that would not have been quite accurate. It was not sexual experience alone she was missing, but something far broader. She exemplified, with clarity, the Revenge of the Un-lived Life, the rejection of whatever possibilities had been open to her as a young woman, the abandonment of love or any strong emotion. She had never exerted her abilities (and she was no fool)

in any direction, but had devoted herself to the care and satisfaction of her selfish mother, to whom she had been a companion and confidant until at last she nursed the old woman into the grave. She was convinced that her mother had been a woman of uncommon intelligence, wisdom, and social correctness, though she never offered me any evidence to justify such an opinion. And now that Mother was dead, she was high and dry without any reason to live.

(278)

This powerful quotation captures the fate of the adult child who remains loyal to the failed parent and who eventually will face the world with a diminished identity and undeveloped interpersonal skills. Note how the novelist demonstrates the idealization found in many such adults: despite her middle age, this character still admired and idealized her selfish mother. This is often the case with many of my patients as well. The parent remains as important, powerful, and wise to them in middle age as they appeared during childhood. Individuals like Miss Fothergill have invested too much time and given up too many of their own possibilities to face the awful reality that faces them as a consequence of their poor choices and childlike misperceptions of their parents—that they have wasted much of their lives.

Searching for Hidden Meanings—Instead of Accepting Bad Luck

Another defensive path that many of my patients take is to try to understand *why* they were not loved or cared for. The search for meaning behind suffering is the result of a defensive insistence that we live in a reasonable and orderly world. Many patients obsess over this question: What did or didn't I do as a child to be treated so badly? When we are rejected by our parents, it seems so deeply personal that we assume there had to be an underlying meaning or reason. However, if we were able to truly find out what the same painful events "meant" to our parents, we would probably be dismayed to discover that the very same events are minimized, distorted, or even worse, long forgotten.

Many parents react to their children from a deep sense of insecurity and jealousy. Dysfunctional parents are not monsters from another planet—rather, they are the last generation of poorly nurtured children (now living in adult bodies) who have been given a role for which they are ill-equipped. When their own insecurity and rage from their deprived childhood histories is coupled with the enormous power and influence they can wield as parents, they can become destructive tyrants. Many use this power in the closed environment of the family to reduce their personal insecurity at the expense of their children. I have been exposed to many such people who reduce their insecurity by abusing others with their superior power, both within the family and in the broader social environment. One of the most notable examples occurred at a dinner to celebrate a scholarly presentation by a visiting professor whose contributions to the field of psychology made him world-famous. The dean of the college and his wife were the hosts for the four of us on the faculty committee who had invited the speaker. During the dinner, the dean's wife began pointedly questioning the guest about his presentation and research. She demanded to know what "gave him the right" to make various claims, despite the fact that she only attended the final twenty minutes of his presentation and had obviously not read any of his papers. The skilled and urbane speaker attempted to defuse this uncomfortable situation with mild and general responses, but the dean's wife persisted. The dean was obviously used to this behavior from his wife and only made one attempt to rebuke her, which she ignored. The dinner proved to be an embarrassment for all, except for the angry wife. On the way out, a colleague who had witnessed the whole painful performance asked me where this woman "got the nerve" to assault the guest speaker with so many irrelevant and hostile questions.

The answer to my colleague's question also answers the question of why so many inept and inadequate parents feel that they have the right to abuse their children in any way they see fit. The answer is that they are so insecure and easily threatened that they strike out at *anyone* who reduces their moment-to-moment sense of comfort. The dean's wife was so insecure about her own worth as a human being that she became angered by the fact that the guest speaker was being celebrated, while she was forced to honor him. Her massive sense of personal worthlessness led her to feel diminished by the public acknowledgment of the speaker's accomplishment. Her questions revealed that she knew absolutely nothing about his research, but that made no difference to her, as she was driven by anxiety, insecurity, and extreme envy—feelings that she discharged on the visiting scholar in an attempt to reduce his stature. By doing so, she was attempting to feel less worthless. She was able to get away with her hostile and demeaning performance because, as hostess and wife of the dean, she was in a powerful position. She was also protected by the social nature of the dinner, which discouraged counteraggression. None of the faculty members were about to take her on in a public and formal situation.

Our parents were in a far more powerful relationship to us than the dean's wife was to the speaker. Many parents are so ill at ease with their children's accomplishments and success, and so fearful of the outside world which has defeated them, that they criticize and diminish their children in order to reduce them to their own level of insecurity. Sadly, when I explain this to my patients, they seldom find that rationale satisfactory. They don't like the impersonal nature of the answer, because it clashes with their memories of how "personal" the attacks from their parents felt. It is difficult for patients to accept that in reality, they were often victimized simply because they happened to be present when their parents insecurity overwhelmed them.

The question as to why we were abused is a continuation of our defenses, in that it assumes there is an inherent logic in life, and that we could have done something differently to please our parents. The ultimate "answer" to the question of why we were rejected, undernurtured, or punished unfairly is simply bad luck—the same bad luck that allows innocent people to be maimed or killed by drunk drivers every year. To continue the analogy, the drunk driver involved in a crippling accident may put the whole incident out of his mind two or three months after the crash, but to the victim who is confined to a wheelchair, the accident will become the central focus of his or her life. We have a great deal of trouble accepting this explanation because it makes the world feel so dangerous, so random, and so lacking in rules.

A powerful example of the search for the "why" behind unjustified abuse is the central question of *My Losing Season*, an emotional and inspired memoir by Pat Conroy, author of a number of novels including *The Prince of Tides* and *The Great Santini*. Conroy's powerful and moving memoir, which captures the torrent of feelings flowing within the abused child, describes his senior year as a college basketball player for the Citadel, a notoriously abusive military academy in Charleston, South Carolina. Conroy's violent childhood prepared him to both tolerate and flourish under the officially sanctioned "plebe" system that encouraged upperclassmen to abuse the freshman class under the assumption that this abuse would serve as an inoculation against emotional breakdown if the cadets were ever captured and brainwashed by enemy forces during their future military careers.

Conroy's father was both physically and psychologically abusive to the point where he would be jailed today if he were caught. Like the dean's wife, Conroy's father was so insecure about his own value that he became enraged whenever anyone else was in the spotlight, most notably his children. The following passage describes a physical attack that Conroy suffered at his father's hands as he was leaving a high school father-son night in which the student athletes were awarded their "letters" for being on the athletic teams:

> Moving slowly with the other student athletes up the carpeted rise toward the milling fathers, I was talking to a boy on my left when I received a stunning backhand across my right jaw that sent me crashing to the floor. The blow was delivered with so much force that I did not know if I was going to be able to rise, but a furor had taken hold of the men above me. Slowly, I rose off my knees and stood on unsteady legs, disoriented, humiliated, and confused by where the blow had come from and why. . . . The second backhand caught me on the left jaw, harder than the first, and I went down to the floor again. (67)

Astonishingly (to the adult raised in a normal family), Conroy helped his father flee from the angry mob of parents who counter-attacked his father for the unjustified beating of his son. Then, in the car on the way home, "it was in this car and on that night that my father took me apart. He gave me a beating like none other I would receive in my childhood" (67). Conroy writes of his abuse with a vividness of detail that conveys the emotions of the child caught in a maelstrom of violence and chaos.

This type of childhood engorges both the wounded self and creates a hopeful self that will inflate little acts of support far beyond their intended meaning. Conroy's real needs for love and support were unmet from his earliest years, so his focus and attachment to any adult who offered the slightest interest was intense. Upon entering the Citadel, Conroy shifted his dependency needs to Mel Thompson, his college coach—a man only marginally better than his father. The question that Conroy struggles with throughout the memoir is why his coach behaved so abusively toward the team, destroying the team's confidence and ruining their entire season. The answer is repetition compulsion. Conroy, by mere happenstance, went to a school where the coach was as brutal as was his father, and Conroy's existing defenses drew him to this coach who had no understanding of how to motivate his players. To Conroy's enduring credit, he followed up on this difficult experience and discovered the truth about the man to whom he was so attached.

Coach Thompson's technique was brutal and impersonal, and he often undermined his very best players. Like Conroy's father, he never ever supported the players with praise: "Mel lacked all gifts or talents required by the language of praise" (156). Even worse, the coach was so demeaning and abusive toward his best players that the "second" team, composed of less-skilled players, would invariably beat the "first" team in scrimmages. The following passage is a quote from one of the first team players whom Conroy interviewed for the book:

> There was absolutely no pressure on the Green Weenies (the second team). We were a lot better than you guys and you knew it.

> We knew there was nothing any of us could do about that. It was
> Mel's great negativity that tore us down. He was a black hole. We
> played badly because he wanted us to play badly.   (162)

During two summers of his college career, Conroy found employ-
ment independently as a counselor at a summer basketball camp
and he was surprised to encounter his coach at the same camp. They
had but one verbal exchange during the two summers he worked
there, despite the fact that Conroy was on Coach Thompson's team
back at the Citadel. "His failure to acknowledge me left me feeling
sullied and insulted, especially when he seemed to relate so well
with the other counselors, the boys from rival colleges" (129).

Despite all the negativity and hostility from Coach Thompson,
Conroy's abusive and abandoning childhood prepared him to become attached to a man whose personality was almost wholly rejecting. The coach made a single supportive gesture during the two
years at basketball camp, and that alone enabled Conroy's hopeful
self to take flight. Conroy had done a spectacular job of defending
against one of the best college scorers in a counselors' game,
which his coach had happened to be watching. As Conroy was
walking back after the game his coach gave him a precious sign of
appreciation:

> Just then someone slapped my fanny, disrupting my reverie. A
> large, dark shape moved past me on the left—Mel Thompson, my
> college coach, smoking, that slap his wordless praise, my reward
> and trophy, and his acknowledgement of the hard work I'd put in
> that summer.   (136)

Thus, Coach Thompson became a new, slightly better (though still
rejecting and abusive) target for all of Conroy's unmet childhood
dependency needs. Despite of all the rejections he and his teammates received from the coach, Conroy, at times, felt an uncanny
sense of attachment and loyalty to him. The following quote comes
at a point in time just after the coach had allowed Conroy to remain on the team after a major infraction: Conroy had burst into

anxiety-driven hysterical laughter during one of Coach Thompson's halftime tirades.

> As I walked slowly to the locker room I was shaken to the core by my urgent and material affection for my coach; no, I was overwhelmed by the profoundness of my own strange loyalty for Mel Thompson. In my life thus far there was nothing odd about this love; love has always issued out of the places that hurt the most, and I feared few men as I feared Mel Thompson. (177)

This loyalty that Conroy describes is a perfect example of Fairbairn's concept of "attachment to bad objects," which is, essentially, all the attachments that I have previously described. Simply stated, the concept of attachment to bad objects describes a child or young adult's attachment to a parent or parent-like individual who frustrates his need for support far more frequently that he or she satisfies that need, while offering just enough real or imagined help to stimulate the hopeful self. The result is an intense need-based attachment that is nearly unshakable. Conroy's hopeful self became attached because he assumed there was love contained in the coach if only he were smart enough and played hard enough to reveal it.

I have noted that the abused child has to develop large wounded self to store and hide all the abuse he has suffered. Often it emerges in violence toward weaker individuals or in self-destructive behaviors. Rarely does the wounded self emerge in ways that are self-enhancing—however, it was Conroy's great fortune that his ability to write allowed him to expose the pathology of his family without hurting himself in the process. He describes a scene where he is returning to college after the Christmas vacation and once again his father is peppering him with insults on the way to the airport. This time his father was demeaning him for not being aggressive enough as a basketball player and for not having "the killer instinct":

> My father was wrong about me. I had the killer instinct, but I called it something else. I called it my first novel. I called it *The*

Great Santini. It would put a cruise missile into his cockpit that
would change my father's life forever.   (210)

Unfortunately, the vast majority of beaten and humiliated children
do not have an outlet for their wounded self that both exposes the
family to external scrutiny and enhances them both in terms of appropriate public empathy and fame. In this powerful memoir Conroy does both.

The single most fascinating aspect of Conroy's memoir is that he
had the courage and insight to test his hypothesis, based on the
moral defense, that there was some logical reason—due to a faulty
characteristic of the players or of the team as a whole—that caused
Mel Thompson's coaching technique to be so demeaning and abusive. Conroy explored his use of the moral defense by visiting and
interviewing his coach thirty years later. Not surprisingly, Coach
Thompson was fired by the Citadel after the 1966 season and had
relocated to the Midwest. Conroy interviewed his coach several
times and found him completely indifferent and disinterested in
everyone on the team and everything that happened:

> But whenever I turned to the year I was writing about, Mel's abil-
> ity to remember the slightest detail deserted him. If I mentioned a
> game, it had slipped from both consciousness and memory. . . .
> When I tried to dig deeply, Mel would answer me with vagueness
> or disinterest until my questions began to sound rude even to me.
> Mel never got angry, he simply seemed not to have lived through
> the same year I had. Where I wore scars, contusions and bruises,
> it seemed not to have laid a single finger on him.   (364–365)

Conroy also noted that his hated, feared, and loved coach asked
him nothing about his life or of the lives of the players who played
their hearts out for him. All Coach Thompson wanted to talk
about were his own college playing years, "so I let him drift back
to his playing days, his glory days in the ACC when he was king of
all he saw" (365). After their second interview, Conroy was joined
by John De Brosse, one of the stars of the 1966 team, for dinner

with the coach. Afterward, Conroy asked Coach Thompson if he wanted to join them for breakfast next morning before they departed. " 'No,' Mel Thompson said, and walked out of my life" (366).

Conroy discovered that it was his bad luck to get this particular coach, who was jealous of his own players, believed that abuse was better than praise, and was more interested in keeping himself in a dominant position by undermining his players confidence, all the while not realizing that these strategies led to the losing season. Again a paradox arises that is common to all forms of failed leadership—no one wanted to win more than Coach Thompson. Unfortunately, like so many parents who are the leaders in the family, the coach was never able to connect his team's failures with his own behavior, just as most parents are honestly unaware that their faulty parenting lead to their children's failures in life. The lesson for all of us is that the abuse we suffer has almost nothing to do with us personally, even if the abuser accuses us of causing the abuse, as Coach Thompson did, and it carries no hidden or special meanings. There was nothing that Conroy or his teammates "did" to his coach to cause the losing season and nothing he or the team as a whole could have done to prevent or to change Coach Thompson's fundamental lack of understanding of his job.

When we speculate about the "why" of our abuse, we are assuming that we were more important to the abuser than we really were, and that we had power to cause events that were, in reality, completely out of our control. Many of our speculations are based on our hopes for hidden love, or the belief that our efforts will change and win over rejecting adults whom we adore. The answer contains no comfort for those looking for order, logic, and a fair and rational universe where good works and efforts are eventually rewarded. Sheldon Kopp, in his book *An End to Innocence*, came to the same conclusion about his experience of childhood abuse—a conclusion that can only be reached after all the defenses that comfort us have been stripped away:

> I realized that though it is probably true that my mother hated me, it was *nothing personal*. Any kid living in that house at that time

would have served as a suitable target. It was my misfortune to
have been the one who wandered in. There was no special meaning to it all, no compensations for that less-than-perfect beginning.

(91)

Amazingly, the conclusion that Kopp reaches, that it was "nothing
personal," is the conclusion that we all must reach to free ourselves
from the bondage of our illusions and defenses. The abuse he received was no more personal than the bodily damage that the victim of a drunk driver receives as a result of a head-on collision. Parents who treat children badly do so out of their own unconscious
pathology, which in turn is based on their own histories, formed
long before their birth. The patient of Joan Raphael-Leff's did
nothing to deserve being treated like a ghost. She "solved" her bad
luck by constructing a network of rescue fantasies that gave her
childhood purpose and hope. Her fantasies were life-saving for her
as a child, but not for her mother. Who knows if her mother wanted to be rescued? Who knows if anyone could have rescued her
mother? The rescue fantasy was never put to the test—rather, it
was designed to keep her psychologically alive during her most vulnerable years. Tragically, the fantasy that comforted her in childhood now enslaves her in adulthood. Her long period of maternal
deprivation undermined her identity and made her fearful and un-
sure of herself in the outside world, and she is left clinging to her
rescue fantasies while her life ticks away.

Accepting Substitute Parents

One positive response to failed parents—one that is easier said than
done—is to leave the conflicting loyalties and resentments behind
and seek out new relationships with those who appreciate us in all
our humanness. Finding a substitute parent to replace the failed
parent often occurs in our society, but it is seldom done with full
consciousness. For instance, there are many stories of wayward,
angry, antisocial young men who have miraculously turned their
lives around because of the influence of a stern but caring coach.

This is the reverse side of the coin described by Conroy; however, the role of coach (just like the role of parent) carries enormous potential both for good or bad. A caring coach is in a position to substitute himself as a better and more appreciative parent. This common human scenario is partially dependent on the size of the wounded self in the young man. If it is too large and too disruptive even the most patient coach will give up. In many instances however, the rage in the wounded self, combined with the thwarted ambition to be loved or at least appreciated, makes the young man a spectacular performer in sports. His aggression and anger find an outlet in physical competition and his hope for love is satisfied by the pride of the coach. The very characteristics which made him "impossible" at home (characteristics that are clearly responses to poor parenting) are suddenly turned into assets on the playing field. We find this common type of story heartening, as it prevents the young man from turning his aggression against innocent people. His attachment to his coach, and the lessons he has learned in terms of sportsmanship (that is, the development of his character) are often applied to society at large.

The re-parenting that goes on between needy children and coaches, teachers, and other available surrogate parents happens largely out of our conscious awareness. However, there are rare occasions when a patient consciously chooses to find a new, better functioning surrogate parent. This happened to a patient of mine, Monica, who had such a paranoid and dangerous mother that she fled her family to save her own sanity. When she was a child, her mother would suddenly jump up and slap her without warning if she was eating too slowly. Her mother also kept the shades drawn because she feared that she was being spied on by the neighbors. Monica's father ignored his wife's peculiarities, as he was often so depressed that he was unable to go to work. By the time Monica came to therapy she was engaged in a dangerous re-creation of her family relationships: she had developed an attachment to a near-criminal boyfriend who was as unpredictable and aggressive as her mother. After a year or so of work in therapy she was able to free herself of the entanglement with her boyfriend. However, she felt the need for a relationship with a "good" mother, a need that I encouraged. As it turned out, she lived in an apartment building that housed both students and retired individuals. One elderly woman seemed particularly happy to visit with Monica whenever they met. They began to shop together on weekends, and then would go out to lunch. Over time they discovered that each gave the other a great deal of pleasure, and their symbolic mother-daughter relationship continued on for many years. This happy result was a consequence of a conscious decision on Monica's part—a rarity, as most of us are too fearful to admit to ourselves that we are leaving our families.

FIVE

Leaving Home

For years I believed that getting my mother to see it my way was
my only hope. It took an awfully long time before I realized that
whether or not she understood, I still could do as I pleased.
Sheldon Kopp

This chapter will detail the process that each of us must go through
to escape the grip of our inhibiting yet still needed family. I have
begun this last chapter with another wise and useful quote from
Sheldon Kopp, who shared the same illusions as many of my patients. Kopp felt that he had to explain himself to his mother and
only when she finally understood him would he be able to be himself. When you are ready to leave home you must be able to tolerate
the reality that your parents will never accept who you really are.
They may argue, threaten, or despair about your decision to leave,
and they may never understand. It is probable that your first step
on the path to self-rescue will be interpreted by your family as
the act of a traitor. The temptation to try to explain yourself to
your parents must be avoided, since imbedded within your efforts
lies the false assumption that they are able to respond to logic and
reason.

Continuing to live in the family home or visiting with parents
daily affords absolutely no chance of emotional development; it
keeps us isolated and alone. Separation from our family of origin
means we must take care of ourselves, and pay our own way in life,

despite the possible inconvenience of a decreased standard of living. Separation from our family in early or middle adulthood requires that we face all of the life tasks that we have postponed.

Accepting the Reality That Separation Is Possible

The very notion that leaving your family is possible or desirable is almost a forbidden thought. It goes against the grain of our human nature and of the values that our culture holds dear. However, it is the essential and self-preserving act that must be taken if we intend to lead a better life. This bold and courageous step can only occur after we conquer our defensive illusions—both about our parents and about ourselves. Our loyalty to our failed parents or to new adult partners who promise love and then frustrate us in familiar ways is the psychological legacy of our incomplete childhood, and these attachments will inexorably keep us from developing a mature and fully functioning identity.

When our parents are elderly and we are middle-aged, the task of separation is formidable, because of the number of years that have passed during which our peers found partners, had children, and created lives for themselves. Many of my patients who remained at home enmeshed in the thrall of their unhappy families have missed many developmental opportunities. As time passes, these tasks and opportunities seem larger and more daunting.

Not only are the external challenges formidable, but our own internal world will also oppose change. Both of our defensive selves will try to thwart the decision to give up the struggle with the family: our hopeful self will continue to spin fantasies of future love and our wounded self will find comfort in hopes for revenge, thus keeping us attached to our rejecting parents. The simple and painful truth is that if a parent (or new partner) has not expressed freely given love after five, ten, or even fifteen years, then love is not available from that person, despite the continuing optimism of the hopeful self. Conversely, our wounded selves will try and convince us to be content with revenge on (or reform of) our rejecting parents or new partners. Defeating the person who refuses to support us will not help in our own personal development as an individual. Neither reform nor revenge is a fulfilling substitute for the consistent love and support that would have allowed us to develop into mature adults. If we are to survive and prosper as adults, we must give up our loyalty to failed parents and rebuild—or build for the first time—our identity by involving ourselves in healthy relationships with supportive others. If we fail, then we will remain trapped by our hopes for illusory love and our equally futile desire for revenge on those who have wronged us.

Most of my patients are fearful of the prospect of facing life without the dubious comfort of their failed families. At the beginning of therapy, many of my patients feel that they will cease to exist without constant contact with their families. The whole idea of giving up on one's family is foreign to human nature, as the following quotation from a patient in treatment with Joan Raphael-Leff from *Narcissistic Wounds* illustrates:

> This is the biggest shock of my life—beyond speech or frantic state—the idea that I don't have to stay with my family forever, that I have a choice. It seems very important to acknowledge how shocking it is—the shame and guilt about my family and how wrong it felt not wanting to stay with them, as though I should have stuck there forever. I'm reeling with the shock of letting something go—a chunk of the past—and facing how few of my needs were ever met. (90)

These are powerful words that illustrate this patient's dawning awareness that she is not condemned to a lifetime of frustration—an awareness that is both rare and unusual in our culture. We are pressured by our dependency needs, by our guilt, our unexpressed rage, and finally by our unrealistic hope into remaining with our families, no matter how badly we were and continue to be treated. The absolute first step on the path to an independent adulthood is to accept the reality that separation is indeed possible and desirable. Many patients fantasize that the family they leave will seek revenge if they begin a separate life of their own. In reality, the source

gth in all unloving families comes from our own unmet de-
ency needs, guilt, and self-created illusions. Once we flee, we
will discover that the family that we feared is completely impotent,
and worse, they may appear to be pathetic when viewed from the
"outside." There are no "family police" to come and arrest us if we
decide to separate and move on in life. The only police we have to
fear are our defenses against seeing how bad life in the family has
been, and our guilt about our failed parents.

Three Pathways to Avoid

The absolutely best advice I received as a young man came from my
high school guidance counselor, who was commenting on my frustration in a class that I had absolutely no interest in. He simply
said, "go where you are wanted and do what works." This is wonderful advice—assuming that you can carry it out. Most of my
adult patients suffering from loyalty to their failed families need a
great deal of support to follow this sage advice. Year after year,
they go where they are not appreciated and try to force others to
love them—often with no success at all. Before we begin discussing
the positive avenues to take for change, I must warn the reader
about three futile strategies that have derailed and delayed improvement in many of my patients. These strategies are seductive,
dangerous, and can often seem like the "natural" or "right" thing
to do, but they can only end up making the attempt at separation
that much more difficult or futile. The following rules regarding
what not to do when beginning to break with failed parents must
be kept in mind.

Rule One: Don't Try to Explain Yourself to Your Jailer

Many patients who spend time in therapy manage to see past their
defenses and experience just how lacking in support or outright destructive their childhoods were. Often, these patients are tempted
to return home and "confront" their parents one last and glorious
time. They crave the opportunity to "face off" with their parents in
order to let them know just how uncaring they were. These patients

mistakenly assume that a dramatic confrontation is a prerequisite to leaving the family.

At first glance, this looks like a bold and healthy course of action. However, upon careful inspection, it is just another reappearance of that old trickster, the wounded self. The wounded self is absolutely dedicated to the false notion that we can get revenge, and that the revenge we obtain will somehow satisfy us—a compelling but entirely false proposition. It is also a venture that will demean us, regardless of the outcome. If we "win," we will probably be faced with the reality of just how sad and unfulfilled are parents are, which can provoke our guilt. What possible good is a victory over such obviously incompetent and pathetic people? On the other hand, if we lose, then we expose ourselves to self-loathing for being intimidated by the powerful tyrants that we still imagine our parents to be. Not only is there nothing to gain from such a victory, but the very act of going back to members of our family to tell them how "bad" they were (and are) is a statement of their continuing importance to us.

Second, achieving a moral victory over failed parents is often a harder task than many of my patients think it to be. Many parents, for whatever reason, simply could not do the job of parenting that they took on but are absolute masters of self-deception. They are absolutely blind to the reality that they are responsible for impeding their child's development. One of my patients described his overtly charming mother as "a mile wide and an inch deep." She could converse with anyone on any topic, and managed to look as if she was a competent and caring mother. Behind closed doors, however, she was crass, arrogant, and abusive. This common type of parent is a formidable opponent, because they are practiced actors whose false and self-serving roles do not produce self-doubt or guilt in them. During confrontations with their wounded children, their confidence makes them impossible to defeat. Today, many of these same parents embrace the popular notion that biological or chemical imbalances, which are clearly not *their* fault, are the source of all of their children's emotional problems. Arguing with a parent like this is akin to arguing against the existence of God at a conference of preachers.

Self-centered and self-righteous parents get their sureness from rigid and absolute views of themselves. This rigidity in their personality structure also prevents them from being sensitive to the needs of others, as all their psychological energy is focused on meeting their own needs. Winning an argument with this type of opponent is simply impossible. I encountered an example of this type of personality in a parent a number of years ago during one of my jobs in a public mental health agency. I was assigned to be the therapist for Brett, a morbidly obese and very depressed sixteen-year-old man who had deliberately cut down twelve of his mother's prized rosebushes at the height of their bloom. One of the most discouraging aspects of working in a public mental health agency is that the parent, who has done the damage to the young person, is often taken more seriously by the agency than is the child. This is because adults can complain and have far more social, legal, and political power and credibility than do their children.

Such was the case with this unfortunate young man, whose mother was the widow of a physician and who was both well-liked and well-known in the community. She presented herself in a dramatic and self-important manner, and ordered the staff to "fix" her son as fast as possible. I was directed to help Brett reconcile with his overbearing and rejecting mother. During my interview with the angry young man, I learned that he had been called a "lazy stuffed sausage" by his mother ever since he could remember. His identity was so damaged and incomplete that he dropped out of high school and spent his days at home working on computers and eating his mother's endlessly offered meals. Like Sheldon Kopp, he was exposed to the emotionally debilitating combination of extreme rejection and constant indulgence. He begged me to intervene on his behalf and implore his mother to stop calling him names. Not surprisingly, the years of deprivation he suffered left him severely psychologically damaged and he had no desire to separate from his mother. His use of the moral defense, along with his hopeful self fantasies, had convinced him that with time and effort he could transform his verbally abusive mother into the parent that he desperately needed. This intense fixation caused him to reject enrollment in a program at the mental health center that was designed to help people like himself develop greater independence. His personality was that of a young child—a child who could not imagine giving up the only mother he knew. All he wanted was to go home to a loving mother who appreciated him.

I recognized that there was no possibility of a healthy reconciliation between this parent and child. The young man's intense dependency (and the extent and power of his wounded self, which caused him to cut down the rosebushes) spoke clearly to me about his history of deprivation. His wounded self was also an experienced revenge plotter, and he described his many strategies for unmasking and defeating his mother, which included hacking into the Web site of the medical society of which his late father was a member and posting hostile statements about his mother's behavior—a very sad way of trying to retaliate against her. Ironically, my position as the young man's therapist required me to interview his mother and inform her of his condition. It seemed to me that reporting to his mother was not in my patient's best interests, but in years past, the rules in public mental health agencies placed considerable emphasis on parental rights. During my interview she demanded to know why her "crazy" son cut her rosebushes down. I diplomatically and vaguely responded that it was a possible indication that he was angry at her. She jumped out of her seat and began to bellow, "Angry at *me*? Angry at ME? What right does he have to be angry at *me*? I have been his servant since he was born!" I could see that I was going to get nowhere with this destructive and self-serving parent. Like many of the parents of my patients, her view of herself was so completely at odds with reality that it was impossible to make any headway. Her absolutely self-centered and rigid view of herself as a "good" parent explained why her desperately dependent son was unable to communicate his frustration using words, finally resorting to cutting down her roses as his only way of indicating his anger and despair. I developed an strategy to deal with Bret within the context of his major interest in life, computers—a strategy that will be detailed later in this chapter.

This example, coupled with literally hundreds of examples from my own practice in which patients tried to confront their parents, has led me to coin the phrase: "Don't complain, and don't explain." That is, don't complain about your emotionally impoverished history to your parents, because they will never validate your perspective of your childhood. Second, don't explain your quiet withdrawal from the family scene. Simply slip away as gracefully as possible and concentrate your efforts at developing relationships with people who support and embrace you.

Rule Two: Don't Wait Around for a "Free Lunch"

Many adults who remain home with their elderly parents rationalize their behavior by saying that they can save money by paying little or no rent, like my patient William, who lived in the basement. Frequently, dysfunctional parents indulge their now-adult children (whom they previously neglected) as a way of keeping them at home. As time passes, the emotionally empty yet superficially indulged adult becomes less motivated to seek success in the outside world. Parental indulgence crushes ambition and stalls the young adult somewhere in middle adolescence. One young woman patient, who had a truly frightening and deprived childhood, returned to her parent's home every weekend (with her dependent husband in tow) to do her laundry, despite the fact that the apartment they lived in had a laundry room. When I asked about her reasons for the weekly trip, during which her mother poured out her woes about being married to an insensitive husband, she claimed that her mother's washing machine did a better job cleaning the clothes! In fact, she could not give up her lifelong efforts to rescue her mother from her aggressive and abusive father. She, like so many other patients, was looking backward to her childhood, instead of forward. Not surprisingly, her neglected marriage dissolved.

The regressive cost of accepting "free" rent can be catastrophic to the already developmentally challenged adult who tries to compensate for past deprivation by selling out his future. Indulgences from parents are extremely seductive precisely because they represent the love that was absent during the child's developmental years. Many of my patients feel that their parents "owe" the free ride because their childhoods were filled with pain. Sadly, indulgences keep the childlike adult dependent and loyal to their frustrating and failed parents, which further reduces the possibility of separation as time goes on.

A dramatic example of the catastrophic consequence of remaining indulgently attached to a frustrating parent was Jason, a middle-aged patient who led a colorful life as an environmental reporter. His freelance articles were highly regarded and brought him considerable fame. He had become well-known in the environmental movement because his personal resources allowed him to investigate water pollution on his own, without being a member of a governmental agency. He was able to pay, out of his own pocket, for tests of samples that he took from industrial wastewater that emptied into public waterways. Jason would then interview the company spokesperson, who most frequently would deny all culpability for polluting. He would then present his results of the testing to the unsuspecting spokesperson, with predictable results. His articles were both pointed and humorous, describing corporate attempts to elude obvious truths. His unconventional tactics would not have been tolerated by establishment newspapers, but his personal resources allowed him a great deal of freedom, and he successfully made a mockery of a number of pompous corporations in the underground press.

Jason came to me for therapy because his personal life was chaotic and unsatisfactory. Most notably, he complained about his weekly telephone "brawl" with his elderly widowed father in Florida. His father had inherited great wealth and had completely abandoned Jason to the care of nursemaids during his childhood, but kept him attached in adulthood by paying most of his bills. Jason's history of being indulged continued on into adulthood, and he rationalized that working at a "normal" job would compromise his creativity, even though his journalistic exploits only took up a fraction of his time. He spent most of his time spinning fantasies of future success with a band of admirers who lived partially off of his largess.

Jason's wounded self displaced his rage away from his powerful and autocratic father and focused it on high-handed corporations who damaged the environment. This served as an outlet for some of the hostility that might have undermined his continuing dependency on his father. Not surprisingly, his history of unmet needs reappeared in his relationships with women. He would become excessively clinging and dependent on one girlfriend after another, most of whom fled because they were not willing to put up with his shrill and demanding behavior.

The focus of my work in therapy with Jason was on the quality of his life at the moment, as well as on the time he was losing because of his insistence on remaining like a child while waiting for his inheritance. He repeatedly told me that his life would change abruptly when his father passed away and he became the inheritor of the family wealth. His fantasy ignored the fact that his damaged identity would remain damaged, even if he did become wealthy. As his therapist, I had hopes for the type of slow, long-term improvement that I have seen in many similar patients. These hopes were dashed by a sudden and unexpected stroke which completely and permanently incapacitated him. His sad fate highlights the dangers of endlessly accepting the role of the dependent "cheated" child who deserves to be indulged as repayment for a failed childhood— our time is short, and interminably waiting around for your problems to be solved is never a good idea.

The loss for all adults who remain loyal to ungiving parents is the loss of time. Living with the attitudes and identity of a child in an adult body is a guaranteed way of wasting time that could be used toward developing a more mature and satisfying way of life. The lost time is simply that—lost—and every passing year reduces the probability that the adult child who remains attached to failed parents will be able to emerge into adulthood.

Rule Three: Don't Overburden Others with Unmet Needs

Many adults reared in unhappy families have few satisfying relationships with peers. There are several interrelated reasons for this. The individual with a damaged identity is often awash in feelings of inferiority, thus making relationships with healthy "others" seem impossible. Conversely, healthy adults expect their relationships with others to operate on a mature give-and-take level. They are not interested in nurturing, cajoling, or endlessly supporting needy friends. As noted, many adults with dysfunctional histories behave in childish ways long into adulthood, and this style of behavior will only be tolerated by similarly emotionally underdeveloped friends.

When individuals from unsupportive families begin anew, they face the danger that their unmet dependency needs will be indiscriminately poured out on everyone. As I have noted in chapter 4, an empty, deprived childhood leaves the young adult painfully needy and self-centered— characteristics that often come out in inappropriate ways. Peer relationships that are normally based on mutual interests and shared sensibilities cannot take the strain imposed if one member approaches the other for endless sympathy and support. Often, middle-aged patients who enter the dating scene after divorce report that a large percentage of the people they meet come at them with excessive and burdensome needs that are completely inappropriate. This can happen on the very first date. The individual who holds out an enormous empty basket of needs expecting them to be met is eliminating the possibility of a relationship with a healthy partner. Healthy individuals are not interested in rescuing desperate peers, nor do they feel guilty about leaving or avoiding excessively demanding acquaintances.

The Pathway to Personal Freedom: Repairing Your Damaged Identity

The great paradox of this book (and of all other self-help books) is the huge gap between reading the book and actually helping oneself. These are two different and widely divergent levels of experience. If we use the narrow definition of the word "self-help," an even greater paradox emerges: *in truth, we cannot really help ourselves*. No child can develop psychologically if he or she is isolated, and the same is true of adults who are developmentally stalled.

Rather, we have to seek out and embrace healthy "others" and allow them to help us mature in the context of mutually rewarding relationships. Our role is to seek out these healthy others, and to participate in groups of people that are bonded to one another by mutual interests.

I have seen a number of patients who attempt to cure themselves by becoming self-help "junkies." They become fascinated with one self-improvement book after another. Many attend experiential workshops year after year, and use the latest and trendiest words including "trauma," "recovery," and "heal" in every other sentence. Despite their voluminous reading, many do not seem to improve because nothing seems to "stick." The missing link between reading a self-help book and actually achieving positive personality growth is a network of long-term give-and-take relationships with concerned others. Human beings simply cannot develop into mature adults (regardless of their chronological age) without the love and support of people around them. When I say "love," I am speaking in the general sense of the word meaning those who appreciate, enjoy, support, and show interest in others.

When a young adult patient comes to a therapist because he or she is living an unfulfilling life at home, the process of becoming independent begins by allowing the patient to shift his or her enormous reservoir of unmet childhood needs away from the failed family and on to the therapist. This is a way of breaking the thrall of dependency that has blinded them for so long. It is simply impossible to physically or emotionally separate from failed parents if you lack a trusted alternative "family" that offers real, rather than illusory, support. This is a task that takes real courage and requires enough trust in the outside world (often in short supply when your own family has failed you) to make the leap. Seeking out the needed support will allow physical separation to occur at a natural and relaxed pace sometime in the future.

Individual therapy is not the only way to shift dependency needs away from the family. Self-help groups, particularly those based on the twelve-step model, do the very same thing. They are able to extend enormous support to all who join while simultaneously demanding very little in return. These groups, though originally only concerned with alcohol abuse, have expanded and cover the effects of faulty parenting as well. They understand the turmoil, fear, and anger that is aroused when one leaves their disappointing family of origin. In either individual therapy or self-help groups, the goal is to seek out and replace our misplaced loyalty and attachment to our failed parents with attachments to healthier peers.

Integrating Our Separate Selves

I have emphasized the role of our defenses in keeping us unaware of the damage that our family has done to us. It is important to be clear as to how the process of therapy or membership in a self-help group repairs the damage done to our identities. For most individuals, the real change comes about when they gradually shift their unmet dependency needs away from their frustrating family and onto the therapist or the self-help group. Therapy allows and encourages this shift, as dependency on the therapist is a natural consequence of revealing yourself to another who is in the role of expert and "helper." This is also true of self-help groups, many of which encourage daily attendance of meetings. Group members shift their frustrated dependency needs away from their families and on to the group, and it becomes in effect a new, better functioning family. Self-help groups can be particularly effective, since they introduce the individual to a community with awareness of and experience with the very issues in which the individual is embroiled. Self-help groups show us that we are not alone, that our reactions to our families are "normal," and that our sense of inferiority is a consequence of the way we were treated and not from personal failure. Groups also allow us to look into the lives of others, some of whom are ahead of us, and some who are behind us in terms of identity development. In effect, they allow us to gauge where we are, how far we have come, and what lies ahead. Another essential property of both personal therapy or self-help groups is that the common problems many immature adults from unloving families display (hypersensitivity to criticism, excessive neediness,

...id cynicism) will not destroy the relationship to either the therapist or the group.

Once the grip of the patient's dependency on his or her family
is broken, the splitting defense can be challenged. Originally, my
patients need both their unrealistic hopeful self and their repressed
wounded self to maintain the attachment to their families. As dependency needs lessen, the influence of the hopeful self fades. The
parent no longer has to be protected by false hopes, because the patient now has access to a better, "parent-like" figure who accepts
him as he is and willingly supports his needs. The relationship helps
the patient assess the merits of his family without the distorting optimism of the hopeful self. Almost every family supported some aspects of their children's development, and it is important that the
patient develops a reality-based view of what his or her family did
and failed to do during his or her developmental years.

Once the illusions of the hopeful self have dissipated, its counterpart, the wounded self, can be addressed. Chapter 4 cautioned
the reader about blindly accepting the intense emotions of the
wounded self as being valid. The therapist's (or the group members') acceptance of the truths contained in the wounded self help
it emerge from the unconscious, and once it is consciously available, it can be "recalibrated." By that, I mean that a realistic discussion of the actual neglect that the patient experienced will allow
the individual to reassess just how bad their childhood really was.
It might have been better or worse that the wounded self
"thought." This new view can reduce the need to act on the emotions that were repressed alongside the memories of parental failures. In some patients, the emotions of rage and terror that occur
when a child is abandoned might involve a wish to kill the neglectful parents. These emotions, though appropriate for the time, remain dangerous if unchanged over years. Discussion of these extreme emotions will often tone them down and allow the patient
better access to his wounded self. Now, he or she no longer has to
fear the loss of his or her family, nor be victimized by the emotions
that it contains. This process results both in a more realistic view
of the extent of the parent's original failures, as well as of their

original goodness. This process also breaks the spell of the moral defense, as the young adult becomes more realistic about what was and was not his or her fault.

The integration of the two once separated selves also goes on in self-help groups, where individual group members tell the story of their lives in the privacy of a group meeting. Members get used to the reality that many of them were abused or neglected, and accept that the shame and the desire to blame oneself is a normal (though unhelpful) reaction to their histories. The integration of the wounded and hopeful self into a single secure identity results in a clear view of the original family that gives the individual a basis for action. This is very different from the extreme and shifting views of the family produced by the unstable selves that prevented change by contradicting any clear action with a sudden opposite view of the family.

The new integrated view often helps patients become realistically aware of how self-centered and insulated from reality their parents really were. This knowledge can be a powerful lever that allows the young adult to separate from his or her family. The following history of Nancy describes a woman whose separation from her mother was so incomplete that she serves as an general example of a typical young adult who failed to differentiate from her neglectful parent.

Nancy was the mother of a six-year-old daughter. She came to see me because of her daily drinking habit, boredom with her limited life, and fear that she was taking too many anti-depressants. Nancy was raised by her mother and stepfather. Her mother was a successful businesswoman and president of the local Chamber of Commerce, who spent a lifetime looking "good" to her friends and neighbors. However, behind closed doors Nancy was the focus of a constant barrage of hostility and aggression from her mother, while her brother was treated with indulgence. When angered, her mother would slap her face until it became numb and then keep Nancy home so the neighbors would not see the swelling. She found no comfort from her stepfather, a man who did nothing to contradict or upset his wife.

Nancy was actively discouraged from applying to college, despite the fact that her mother, stepfather, and brother were all college graduates. The anger and alienation in her wounded self emerged in high school, where she became sexually promiscuous. Her behavior was both a rebellion against her abusive mother and a desperate search for someone who would love her. Not surprisingly, she became pregnant and married hastily. She and her husband moved to a town two hours away from her family home, and Nancy became severely depressed. She displayed the typical paradoxical response of the undernurtured, dependent young adult: despite the animosity she felt for her mother, she could not tolerate living far away from her, as her childhood needs still cried out for satisfaction. Nancy pressured her husband to return to her hometown, and they found a house just blocks away from her abusive mother. As in so many other cases, Nancy remained dependent on the mother who thwarted her emotional development. They spoke several times a day and her mother's opinions dominated her life. At times, it seemed that her entire identity was being taken over by her intrusive and omnipotent mother.

When we began our work, Nancy appropriately felt that life was passing her by. The world outside the narrow confines of her home seemed exciting, but it also frightened her. Her first attempt to venture out was as a door-to-door sales person for beauty products, but the large number of rude rejections discouraged her and she ended up keeping most of the stock herself. As she progressed in therapy, she recognized that even her home was not safe, since she invited her mother over frequently. Nancy often felt that her mother wanted to control all aspects of her life. Despite her best attempts to separate during the first year of work in therapy, she continued to call her mother morning and night to report the day's events.

Nancy gradually became more emotionally attached to me and this allowed her to slowly pull away from her mother during the second year of therapy. She no longer called her mother daily, maintaining a reasonable distance while simultaneously developing her own resources. The emotional support that she gained from our work allowed her to take a part-time job in retail sales, and she found (much to her surprise) that she often won the store's monthly sales contest because of her ebullience and ability to respond warmly to a wide variety of customers. Her job became full-time, which made child-care a far more important issue, and Nancy reversed her attempts to avoid her mother, because she needed help watching her daughter. This brought her back into daily contact with her mother, which was a temporary negative setback that was paradoxically prompted by positive growth in her personality.

There was a clear difference in Nancy's view of her mother when they resumed contact, as therapy allowed her hopeful and wounded selves to merge in a stronger, more realistic, and confident identity. She became more and more aware of just how much of her mother's hostile behavior she had learned to excuse or ignore. Finally, at Christmas dinner she could no longer keep up the charade. She and her family were seated at a card table in an alcove while her mother, stepfather, and brother entertained their friends at the main table. Her work with me had given her courage to see and to voice her pain when she was ill-used. The crisis came the next day when she dropped by her mother's house with her daughter to retrieve a serving plate. Her mother remarked that Christmas dinner had been a complete success. Nancy uncharacteristically responded that it was a complete waste of time for her, because she had been treated as second-class citizen. She also vowed to celebrate all future holidays with her own family to avoid any possibility of similar future humiliations.

This was the first time in her adult life that she told her mother directly how she felt about being demeaned. It was made possible by her attachment to me as a "new" parent which allowed her to risk losing her frustrating one. Her newly integrated identity no longer relied upon a wounded self that repressed all of her mother's insults or a hopeful self that urged her to try and win her mother's (assumed) love. Not surprisingly, her mother became enraged, as she was not used to being challenged by a daughter toward whom she had spent a lifetime expressing contempt. Her mother immediately counterattacked, saying that Nancy was an ingrate and a "spoiled brat" who was lucky to be invited for the holidays. Instead of backing down, Nancy reminded her mother of the many incidents of abuse that she remembered from her childhood. This made her mother more enraged and the commotion in the living room attracted her brother, who came racing to his mother's rescue. Nancy's brother had no steady job and lived in an apartment in the basement of the house. He stormed up the stairs to see his desperately needed mother in a verbal battle with his low-status sister. He shared the family contempt for Nancy, and the fact that she had the nerve to upset their mother threw him into a rage. He began pushing her out the door, and as a gesture intended to completely demean her, spat on her in front of her child.

The drama symbolized the way that Nancy was regarded by the whole family, and it was exactly what she needed to convince her to separate once and for all from her family. This event was only able to occur because her integrated identity no longer hid from reality. Instead of using the moral defense and accepting the "bad" label that her family tried to place on her for causing the commotion, she used the event to explain to her daughter that it was the reason that they were no longer going to visit. This event focused her emotional needs on me and the AA group that she attended. Her resolve to separate, supported by her attachment to me and to her group, allowed her to remain independent.

The Pathway to Personal Freedom:
Joining a Special Interest Group

The second part of the process of individuation begins when the dependency issues have been somewhat resolved and the individual is ready to work on improving his or her social skills and expanding his or her interpersonal network. This requires each individual to assess his or her talents and interests in topics, issues, or movements that are larger than themselves and join a "special interest" group that shares those interests and requires nothing more from the patient than enthusiasm. I often help patients in this process by asking them about the magazines they read. Every specialty magazine, from body building to politics, from cameras to motorcycles, from ro... climbing to gardening, has both local and national organizations staffed by people who are similarly focused on that specific interest. Special interest groups allow us to become personally involved and invested in relating to the world in a less self-centered manner. Membership in specific interest organizations also tends to diffuse our selfish concerns and replace them with concerns about larger issues and also, with concerns about the other members of the group. These new groups are not intended to replace the self-help group or personal therapy. Rather, they should continue to serve as a relational foundation that supports the individual during his or her exploration of the larger world. The more interpersonal networks one has, the better and richer life will be. The new relationships with healthy peers will support and sustain us long into the future.

This was the tactic that I took with Brett, the overweight young man who cut down his mother's roses. Brett had developed computer programming skills and was an accomplished hacker. He also repaired computers and wrote software. Despite these interests, he was firmly attached to his destructive mother. Brett's history with his mother made him a wary and difficult patient, one who resisted therapy to the point where he often wore me down. However, I noticed that his interests in computers vitalized him in a way that nothing else had the power to do. I changed my therapeutic strategy from psychotherapy to a form of "occupational" therapy. First, I suggested that he join a local computer interest group, but I soon learned that there were none that met face to face. His computer peers were psychologically similar, socially isolated hackers, with whom he communicated on the Internet and never met in person. I then asked Brett to help me learn about various aspects of the computer, as I was a complete novice. This request surprised him—it was a role reversal and no one of any importance had ever asked him for help. I was joined by another member of the staff who was as computer illiterate as I, and Brett became our teacher. We paid him a nominal fee, and he successfully introduced us to the world of word processing. He was then asked to help our publicity and information specialist, who also paid him. Within several months, he had expanded his "customer base" to include the computer needs of other parts of the mental health center, including its two halfway houses and its supervised apartment network. He spent more and more time away from his mother and began earning money for the first time in his life. One of the outreach workers found a storefront and helped Brett rent it from the owner, in which he set up a computer repair shop, while continuing to work for the mental health center. In effect, the mental health center served as a new family, one that appreciated his talents and accomplishments. He eventually moved out of his house and into an apartment and continued to succeed in his small business venture. Brett's success attracted a number of younger, similarly neglected young men who began spending time at his shop and he moved from the position of a "help receiver" to a "help giver." He served as a model for these young men and over a few years his interpersonal and social skills matured remarkably. Brett is an example of an individual whose damaged identity (specifically, his wariness of anyone in a parental role) prevented him from accepting help from conventional therapy, but who improved greatly by developing his interests and skills in the benevolent atmosphere of a new family. He developed enough confidence to separate from his mother, and now leads an independent life of his own making.

Brett didn't join a special interest group; he created one around himself, and the positive effect was the same. It is absolutely necessary for each of us to reach out to others with similar interests as a way of developing a healthy network of friendships. Every group or club, be it political, social, environmental, musical, or recreational contains healthy individuals. The task of the adult who is separating from his family is to bring his enthusiasm and interest to the organization, while leaving his wounded self in the past, letting the natural course of relating to others unfold.

How Much Separation from Your Family Is Enough?

The examples that I have used so far to illustrate unhappy families vary in regard to the intensity of faulty parenting to which they subjected their children. Simply put, not all unhappy families are equally destructive, and thus, the act of separating from them will depend on how much each individual can tolerate knowing how severely his particular family failed him or her during childhood. A second issue is how much time the now stronger young adult can tolerate spending time with his family in the present. The issue of obligation varies from family to family—how much we "owe" our families after our own unresolved dependency needs are removed— is not the same in every family. Therefore, when I speak of separation from our family of origin, I am not speaking in absolutes. For some of us, occasional visits are fine; for others, perhaps phone contact is all that is tolerable.

I will return to number of patients that I have described in previous chapters, and note how they managed to accommodate their need for independence along with their sense of obligation to their family of origin. Terry, my patient from chapter 1 who owned the wine and specialty food shops, made slow and constant progress over a three-year course of therapy. As a young adult she had allowed her mother to become her sole support, and her work with me altered that relationship dramatically. Terry and I spent a great deal of time trying to develop a realistic picture of her mother as a parent, as Terry felt obligated to behave toward her mother in a manner that was morally appropriate. Our discussion revealed that Terry and her two brothers (who were estranged from their demanding and infantile mother) were raised under conditions of "benign neglect." They were fed and clothed, but their mother simply was too preoccupied with her own needs to pay any attention to her children's needs for tenderness, comfort, or support. Terry and I discussed, over and over again, the "right" thing to do. Over the years in therapy, Terry's two brothers, who had ignored her in the past because she and their mother behaved as a single unit, came to rely on Terry to mediate the family obligations toward their mother. She negotiated a plan for her mother to be placed in a nursing home with the financial assistance from her brothers, who were relieved that Terry had become a responsible agent in her own right. These negotiations opened up lines of contact between her brothers and herself and she regained parts of her family that she had previously lost. She no longer tolerated her mother's infantile behavior and became increasingly protective of herself around her mother. This had the unexpected consequence of bringing her closer to her brothers and their families. Terry treated her increasingly elderly mother as the child she had always been. She visited her mother occasionally in the nursing home, but focused her energy on management of her mother's care, rather than attempting to involve herself emotionally, echoing the way that she herself was raised. She maintained her new relationship with her brothers and expanded her two businesses. Her increased availability and her reduced fear of friendships expanded her social network as a natural consequence of her business contacts, though at our termination the "man problem" remained.

Terry illustrates a common problem faced by adults who finally separate from their dysfunctional families in middle age, which is to what extent should they become involved in late-life care for their parents. The great temptation for many of my patients is to use this opportunity to finally "get close" to their parent or parents. I often suggest to my patients that the emotionally appropriate response to the care of an elderly parent should be based on the type of childhood that their parent provided for them as a child. Those parents who were sadistic or malicious toward them during childhood are obviously not deserving of special care, though in the paradoxical world of unmet dependencies, this type of parent is often given the greatest consideration. Again, what motivates this behavior is the undernurtured adult's attempt to get the closeness (even though the closeness originates in them, not in the parent) that was not given to them in childhood. Katherine Harrison's description of her care of her dying mother in *Thicker Than Water* illustrates this common psychological scenario. Parents who were inattentive and incompetent rather than actively malicious deserve greater consideration. My experience suggests that most emotionally deprived adults who mistakenly view the situation as an opportunity to get the closeness that they were deprived of in childhood are disappointed with the results. Another factor that further precludes a rational response to the once neglectful elderly parent by the still dependent child is the reality that the self-centered parent who failed to nurture their child most often becomes a more demanding, insistent, and guilt-producing elder than do older parents who were emotionally supportive toward their children. Thus we have a emotionally weaker adult who still craves closeness facing an elderly parent who is that much more aggressive and demanding. Understandably, many of my patients try to make up for a lifetime of deprivation late in their parent's lives.

William, the failed teacher who lived in the basement of his parent's home, was a greater challenge as a patient than was Terry, because his transferences (his emotional habits transferred to me from his relationship with his parents) were so severe that they threatened to disrupt our working alliance. Initially, I developed the "baseball scoring" game to reduce the sting of the hostility that William poured out on me. William's wounded self was developed in relationship to his intellectual but harshly critical European parents, and it was filled to the brim with spite and sadistic pleasure at my discomfort. Naturally, William was only passing on to me what had been done to him in childhood, but this knowledge did little to reduce the anger that I felt when attacked by him. His hostile and cynical style made outside relationships impossible, and so our first goal was to reduce his self-destructive transferences. Interestingly, William had an enormous wounded self, but I could see no signs of a hopeful self; that is, he had no illusions of love in the future from his parents or from anyone else. During our work in therapy, he became coldly cynical toward his parents, saying that he would stay in their house as long as they paid the rent. Much of our work focused on his enormous hostility toward me. He rationalized his behavior by saying that I was a professional who was paid to take abuse. In reality, I found his abuse nearly intolerable, and my skills at reducing defenses were being severely tested. In 1989, I was involved in an auto accident that left me bruised and stiff, but with no broken bones. I continued to see my patients despite moderate to severe back pain. To my amazement, William almost broke down in tears during the first session that we met after my accident.

He was absolutely aghast when he saw me and could hardly speak. I realized that he had shifted his dependency needs onto me, but these attachments were deeply hidden behind the thick curtain of his hostility. He felt that I was his last hope (as few peers or friends came knocking on his basement door) and were he to lose me, he would forego the only way out of his dilemma. During that first post-accident session I noted that he was surprisingly short of his normal "patter" and all he could do in response was stare at me with despair in his eyes. This dramatic event broke the endless attacks on me, and we began to discuss the contents of his wounded self. That is, we reviewed the specifics of his parents failures to nurture and support him during his developmental years. This discussion took many months, during which time we also developed a strategy to cope with William's psychological damage. Luckily for both of us, William had not lost his interest in music—in fact, one of his wounded self's strategies to get his parents angry was to play jazz on his saxophone late into the night. Not surprisingly, his parents hated jazz, regarding it as more evidence that American culture was inferior to European culture. I was wary of making any overt suggestions to William, as he continued to resist all suggestions— though not with his previously displayed sarcasm. I assumed that over time our relationship would reduce the sensitivity, fear, and hostility in his wounded self, and when that came under control he would be able to take advantage of those few opportunities that came his way. I had guessed that his music would lead him out of the basement, and his "big break" did eventually come in the form of a two-week job as a substitute music teacher in a nearby school. Luckily, it was not the same school in which he had his depressive reaction to the rejection of his teaching program two years before. He was surprised at the warm reception he received from his teaching colleagues, and was invited to go to a Friday afternoon "happy hour." Prior to our work, he would have rejected the invitation offhand. Now, however, the reduction of his sensitivity and wariness allowed him to accept. As in many of my patients, one thing led to another, and William began substitute teaching on a regular basis and later joined a local jazz trio that played on weekends. Our real

focus was on how he could leave home and how to better relate t
his parents, whom he viewed alternately with contempt, pity, dis-
gust, and sadness. Over several years and many hours in my consulting room, William worked out a plan of separation from them
that involved buying a condo and visiting his parents on holidays.
He tried to keep his hostility toward them to a minimum, and he
established a rule (that his parents initially ridiculed), which stated
that he would leave their house the moment they began to criticize
American culture or his life. It only took one instance of his leaving to convince them that he had enough strength to carry out his
rule. His reduced dependency on them, along with his relationship
with me and his new network of friends, offered him enough support to carry out his promise to leave.

Sandy, my patient who used the splitting defense so frequently
that it disrupted one friendship after another, came to a different
conclusion regarding continued contact with her family. Sandy's
treatment involved our working on her use of splitting in the therapy hour. She came in after reading my book *The Illusion of Love*,
saying that she didn't want to waste any time and was only willing
to talk to a "top-notch" person. Whenever a patient idealizes me
(that is, when a patient sees me from the hopeful self), I immediately become alert to the probability that they are using the splitting defense. Once I am idealized, I know that a sudden devaluation is just around the corner. Sandy was an intellectual
powerhouse, so I approached her as if she were a colleague and explained to her the process of splitting. I tried to preempt a wounded self attack and offered her insights into the ways that her personality operated. I urged her to keep an eye out for her wounded
self—particularly in regards to a sudden devaluation of me. I mentioned this possibility while she was in her hopeful self, and she
could not believe that she would ever see me in a negative manner—after all I was "top-notch."

Note that my approach to any given patient varies given their individual characteristics. I would have never taken this approach
with Brett, the computer hacker, who resisted all my efforts, or with
William, who would have mocked any explanation of personality

functions. Sandy, however, was curious and interested in psychological functioning, and we developed a powerful alliance. One afternoon she called my answering service and excitedly reported that she had split into her wounded self because after our session she began to see me as a fraud and charlatan. Rather than taking her sudden devaluation of me seriously, she was observing herself from a distance. She even noted that she wanted to work her new understanding of psychology into one of her screenplays. Sandy's work with me proceeded rapidly because of her cooperation and willingness to explore the functioning of her personality and because she was able to look at—rather than act out—her defenses. We reviewed her history of flare-ups with her friends and traced the frustrations or losses that provoked her to switch from her hopeful self to her wounded self. She wrote several letters of apology to the friends that she had become suddenly angry with, though (wisely) she did not go into the details of why she got so angry. We spent a good deal of time reviewing her relationship with her abusive mother and exploitative sister, and we discussed how her need of them could so swiftly shift into contempt. Sandy concluded that her mother's physical and emotional abuse of her as a child gave her the right to drop all concerns for her and simply remain in infrequent phone contact. She was able to follow the rule "never complain, never explain" and much to her surprise, her mother never even noticed the decrease in interaction. Sandy continued to work on integrating her identity and eventually began to date once again.

Finally, Gary, the grandiose undergraduate who sued the university, needed no help separating from his family, since he was already living on his own. His issues (like William's) involved his overactive wounded self, as he often antagonized others in authority positions. He initially came for therapy just after his graduation because of a severe depression caused by the sudden drop in his status—he lost his self-definition as a student-celebrity who was "fighting" for student rights. We worked well for several years and then terminated. Gary worked for a timber harvesting company and learned to love the forest. He became skilled in the use of chainsaws and learned the principles of good forestry. He was a member of an outdoor club and returned to therapy because he was in considerable difficulty with a number of the most prominent and senior members. Gary related to the club officers in the same way he related to the university—namely, he argued with nearly all the decision they made. Unlike the university setting, where decorum was a way of life, a number of the older men in the hiking club took him aside after a meeting and suggested that he "get lost." This powerful confrontation faced him with more direct aggression than he was used to. Like most angry young men with large wounded selves, he was used to dishing out abuse but very sensitive when it came back his way. This difficulty was the crack in his defenses that I needed, as for the first time Gary acknowledged that he needed my help. He had developed attachments to the club and enjoyed both the organized hikes and the sense of belonging that he got from being a member. He viewed conservation of the forest as a priority and respected others who shared this view, though he had been unable to control the hostility in his wounded self. He had damaged his reputation quite thoroughly in a short period of time, and we looked at ways that he might regain the goodwill of his fellow members.

The answer we came up with was to make use of Gary's woodland skills. Each spring, the club devoted a full month to trail improvements and shelter repairs, as the heavy snows and cold temperatures inevitably did a great deal of damage to the overnight shelters on the trail. Gary accepted my suggestion to volunteer as the manager of a shelter rebuilding project, one that required that he spend several weekends in the remote site. This appealed to his romance with the forest and also harnessed his forestry and building skills. It also for the first time in his life put him in the position of authority (rather than of a criticizer), and he was surprised at how defensive he became when any aspect of "his" project was criticized. Gary gave back to an organization that was about to send him on his way, and this reversal won back the goodwill of a number of his prior detractors and deepened his commitment and strengthened his social network.

These examples illustrate that there are many ways of leaving one's family of origin, and that simple separation is often not enough. Healing the damage done to us by our own childhood defenses is as important as physically and emotionally separating from our family. Progress is not always linear, and there are often unforeseen setbacks. However, the process can be resumed again and again until one reaches the goal of creating a supportive network of friendships. The setbacks that occur are to be expected, but in the long run, the development of a new and healthy network of relationships while simultaneously leaving frustrating family attachments is the key task in living a good and satisfying life.

REFERENCES

Celani, D. 1993. *The Treatment of the Borderline Personality: Applying Fairbairn's Object Relations Theory in the Clinical Setting.* Madison, Conn.: International Universities Press.

———. 1994. *The Illusion of Love: Why the Battered Woman Returns to Her Abuser.* New York: Columbia University Press.

Conroy, P. 2002. *My Losing Season.* New York: Bantam Books.

Davies, R. 1995. *The Cunning Man.* New York: Penguin Books.

Du Plessix–Gray, F. 1995. "Starving Children." *The New Yorker,* 16 October, 51.

Fairbairn, W. R. D. 1952. *Psychoanalytic Studies of the Personality.* Boston: Routledge & Kegan Paul.

Goodwin, D. K. 1994. *No Ordinary Time.* New York: Touchstone Books.

Harrison, K. 1991. *Thicker Than Water.* New York: Random House.

———. 1997. *The Kiss.* New York: Random House.

Kopp, S. 1978. *An End to Innocence: Facing Life Without Illusions.* New York: Bantam Books.

Laing, R. D. 1969. "The Family and the 'Family.' " In Laing, *The Politics of the Family.* New York: Random House.

Lawson, C. 2000. *Understanding the Borderline Mother.* Northvale, N.J.: Jason Aronson.

Leo, J. 1981. "A Sad Baffling Dependency." *Time*, 6 April, 45.

Miller, A. 1983. *For Your Own Good: Hidden Cruelty in Child-Rearing and the Roots of Violence.* New York: Farrar Straus Giroux.

Porter, K. A. 1970. "The Necessary Enemy." In *The Collected Essays and Occasional Writings of Katherine Ann Porter.* Boston: Houghton Mifflin.

Raphael-Leff, J. 1995. "Narcissistic Displacement in Childbearing." In *Narcissistic Wounds*, edited by J. Cooper and N. Maxwell. Northvale, N.J.: Jason Aronson.

Wilson, P. 1995. "Narcissism and Adolescence." In *Narcissistic Wounds*, edited by J. Cooper and N. Maxwell. Northvale, N.J.: Jason Aronson.

INDEX